PASSAGE

to

INDIA.

Gliding o'er all, through all,
Through Nature, Time, and Space,
As a Ship on the waters advancing,
The Voyage of the Soul—not Life alone,
Death—many Deaths, I sing.

Fredonia Books
Amsterdam, The Netherlands

Passage to India

by
Walt Whitman

ISBN: 1-4101-0721-3

Reprinted from the 1870 edition

Fredonia Books
Amsterdam, The Netherlands
http://www.fredoniabooks.com

In order to make original editions of historical works available to scholars at an economical price, this facsimile of the original edition of 1870 is reproduced from the best available copy and has been digitally enhanced to improve legibility, but the text remains unaltered to retain historical authenticity.

PASSAGE

to

INDIA.

Gliding o'er all, through all,
Through Nature, Time, and Space,
As a Ship on the waters advancing,
The Voyage of the Soul—not Life alone,
Death—many Deaths, I sing.

CONTENTS.

iv CONTENTS.

Passage to India.

—

1

[1] Singing my days,
Singing the great achievements of the present,
Singing the strong, light works of engineers,
Our modern wonders, (the antique ponderous Seven
    outvied,)
In the Old World, the east, the Suez canal,
The New by its mighty railroad spann'd,
The seas inlaid with eloquent, gentle wires,
I sound, to commence, the cry, with thee, O soul,
The Past! the Past! the Past!

[2] The Past! the dark, unfathom'd retrospect!
The teeming gulf! the sleepers and the shadows!
The past! the infinite greatness of the past!
For what is the present, after all, but a growth out of
    the past?
(As a projectile, form'd, impell'd, passing a certain line,
    still keeps on,
So the present, utterly form'd, impell'd by the past.)

2

[3] Passage, O soul, to India!
Eclaircise the myths Asiatic—the primitive fables.

[4] Not you alone, proud truths of the world!
Nor you alone, ye facts of modern science!
But myths and fables of eld—Asia's, Africa's fables!

The far-darting beams of the spirit!—the unloos'd
    dreams!
The deep diving bibles and legends ;
The daring plots of the poets—the elder religions ;
—O you temples fairer than lilies, pour'd over by the
    rising sun!
O you fables, spurning the known, eluding the hold of
    the known, mounting to heaven!
You lofty and dazzling towers, pinnacled, red as roses,
    burnish'd with gold!
Towers of fables immortal, fashion'd from mortal
    dreams!
You too I welcome, and fully, the same as the rest ;
You too with joy I sing.

3

⁵ Passage to India!
Lo, soul! seest thou not God's purpose from the first ?
The earth to be spann'd, connected by net-work,
The people to become brothers and sisters,
The races, neighbors, to marry and be given in mar-
    riage,
The oceans to be cross'd, the distant brought near,
The lands to be welded together.

⁶ (A worship new, I sing ;
You captains, voyagers, explorers, yours!
You engineers! you architects, machinists, yours !
You, not for trade or transportation only,
But in God's name, and for thy sake, O soul.)

4

⁷ Passage to India!
Lo, soul, for thee, of tableaus twain,
I see, in one, the Suez canal initiated, open'd,
I see the procession of steamships, the Empress Euge-
    nie's leading the van ;
I mark, from on deck, the strange landscape, the pure
    sky, the level sand in the distance ;

I pass swiftly the picturesque groups, the workmen
    gather'd,
The gigantic dredging machines.

8 In one, again, different, (yet thine, all thine, O soul,
    the same,)
I see over my own continent the Pacific Railroad, sur-
    mounting every barrier ;
I see continual trains of cars winding along the Platte,
    carrying freight and passengers ;
I hear the locomotives rushing and roaring, and the
    shrill steam-whistle,
I hear the echoes reverberate through the grandest
    scenery in the world ;
I cross the Laramie plains—I note the rocks in gro-
    tesque shapes—the buttes ;
I see the plentiful larkspur and wild onions—the bar-
    ren, colorless, sage-deserts ;
I see in glimpses afar, or towering immediately above
    me, the great mountains—I see the Wind River
    and the Wahsatch mountains ;
I see the Monument mountain and the Eagle's Nest—
    I pass the Promontory—I ascend the Nevadas ;
I scan the noble Elk mountain, and wind around its
    base ;
I see the Humboldt range—I thread the valley and
    cross the river,
I see the clear waters of Lake Tahoe—I see forests of
    majestic pines,
Or, crossing the great desert, the alkaline plains, I be-
    hold enchanting mirages of waters and meadows ;
Marking through these, and after all, in duplicate slen-
    der lines,
Bridging the three or four thousand miles of land
    travel,
Tying the Eastern to the Western sea,
The road between Europe and Asia.

9 (Ah Genoese, thy dream ! thy dream !
Centuries after thou art laid in thy grave,
The shore thou foundest verifies thy dream !)

5

[10] Passage to India!
Struggles of many a captain—tales of many a sailor
        dead!
Over my mood, stealing and spreading they come,
Like clouds and cloudlets in the unreach'd sky.

[11] Along all history, down the slopes,
As a rivulet running, sinking now, and now again to
        the surface rising,
A ceaseless thought, a varied train—Lo, soul! to thee,
        thy sight, they rise,
The plans, the voyages again, the expeditions :
Again Vasco de Gama sails forth ;
Again the knowledge gain'd, the mariner's compass,
Lands found, and nations born—thou born, America,
        (a hemisphere unborn,)
For purpose vast, man's long probation fill'd,
Thou, rondure of the world, at last accomplish'd.

6

[12] O, vast Rondure, swimming in space!
Cover'd all over with visible power and beauty!
Alternate light and day, and the teeming, spiritual
        darkness ;
Unspeakable, high processions of sun and moon, and
        countless stars, above ;
Below, the manifold grass and waters, animals, moun-
        tains, trees ;
With inscrutable purpose—some hidden, prophetic
        intention ;
Now, first, it seems, my thought begins to span thee.

[13] Down from the gardens of Asia, descending, radiat-
        ing,
Adam and Eve appear, then their myriad progeny after
        them,
Wandering, yearning, curious—with restless explo-
        rations.

With questionings, baffled, formless, feverish—with
    never-happy hearts,
With that sad, incessant refrain, *Wherefore, unsatisfied*
    Soul? and, *Whither, O mocking Life?*

[14] Ah, who shall soothe these feverish children?
Who justify these restless explorations?
Who speak the secret of impassive Earth?
Who bind it to us? What is this separate Nature, so
    unnatural?
What is this Earth, to our affections? (unloving earth,
    without a throb to answer ours;
Cold earth, the place of graves.)

[15] Yet, soul, be sure the first intent remains—and shall
    be carried out;
(Perhaps even now the time has arrived.)

[16] After the seas are all cross'd, (as they seem already
    cross'd,)
After the great captains and engineers have accomplish'd
    their work,
After the noble inventors—after the scientists, the
    chemist, the geologist, ethnologist,
Finally shall come the Poet, worthy that name;
The true Son of God shall come, singing his songs.

[17] Then, not your deeds only, O voyagers, O scientists
    and inventors, shall be justified,
All these hearts, as of fretted children, shall be sooth'd,
All affection shall be fully responded to—the secret
    shall be told;
All these separations and gaps shall be taken up, and
    hook'd and link'd together;
The whole Earth—this cold, impassive, voiceless Earth,
    shall be completely justified;
Trinitas divine shall be gloriously accomplish'd and
    compacted by the true Son of God, the poet,
(He shall indeed pass the straits and conquer the
    mountains.

He shall double the Cape of Good Hope to some pur-
     pose ;)
Nature and Man shall be disjoin'd and diffused no more,
The true Son of God shall absolutely fuse them.

<h2 style="text-align:center">7</h2>

[18] Year at whose open'd, wide-flung door I sing!
Year of the purpose accomplish'd!
Year of the marriage of continents, climates and
     oceans!
(No mere Doge of Venice now, wedding the Adriatic ;)
I see, O year, in you, the vast terraqueous globe, given,
     and giving all,
Europe to Asia, Africa join'd, and they to the New
     World ;
The lands, geographies, dancing before you, holding a
     festival garland,
As brides and bridegrooms hand in hand.

<h2 style="text-align:center">8</h2>

[19] Passage to India!
Cooling airs from Caucasus far, soothing cradle of man,
The river Euphrates flowing, the past lit up again.

[20] Lo, soul, the retrospect, brought forward ;
The old, most populous, wealthiest of Earth's lands,
The streams of the Indus and the Ganges, and their
     many affluents ;
(I, my shores of America walking to-day, behold, resum-
     ing all,)
The tale of Alexander, on his warlike marches, suddenly
     dying,
On one side China, and on the other side Persia and
     Arabia,
To the south the great seas, and the Bay of Bengal ;
The flowing literatures, tremendous epics, religions,
     castes,
Old occult Brahma, interminably far back—the tender
     and junior Buddha,
Central and southern empires, and all their belongings,
     possessors,

The wars of Tamerlane, the reign of Aurungzebe,
The traders, rulers, explorers, Moslems, Venetians,
    Byzantium, the Arabs, Portuguese,
The first travelers, famous yet, Marco Polo, Batouta
    the Moor,
Doubts to be solv'd, the map incognita, blanks to be
    fill'd,
The foot of man unstay'd, the hands never at rest,
Thyself, O soul, that will not brook a challenge.

9

[21] The medieval navigators rise before me,
The world of 1492, with its awaken'd enterprise ;
Something swelling in humanity now like the sap of
    the earth in spring,
The sunset splendor of chivalry declining.

[22] And who art thou, sad shade?
Gigantic, visionary, thyself a visionary,
With majestic limbs, and pious, beaming eyes,
Spreading around, with every look of thine, a golden
    world,
Enhuing it with gorgeous hues.

[23] As the chief histrion,
Down to the footlights walks, in some great scena,
Dominating the rest, I see the Admiral himself,
(History's type of courage, action, faith ;)
Behold him sail from Palos, leading his little fleet ;
His voyage behold—his return—his great fame,
His misfortunes, calumniators—behold him a prisoner,
    chain'd,
Behold his dejection, poverty, death.

[24] (Curious, in time, I stand, noting the efforts of
    heroes ;
Is the deferment long? bitter the slander, poverty,
    death ?
Lies the seed unreck'd for centuries in the ground ?
    Lo! to God's due occasion,

Uprising in the night, it sprouts, blooms,
And fills the earth with use and beauty.)

10

²⁵ Passage indeed, O soul, to primal thought !
Not lands and seas alone—thy own clear freshness,
The young maturity of brood and bloom ;
To realms of budding bibles.

²⁶ O soul, repressless, I with thee, and thou with me,
Thy circumnavigation of the world begin ;
Of man, the voyage of his mind's return,
To reason's early paradise,
Back, back to wisdom's birth, to innocent intuitions,
Again with fair Creation.

11

²⁷ O we can wait no longer !
We too take ship, O soul !
Joyous, we too launch out on trackless seas !
Fearless, for unknown shores, on waves of extasy to
    sail,
Amid the wafting winds, (thou pressing me to thee, I
    thee to me, O soul,)
Caroling free—singing our song of God,
Chanting our chant of pleasant exploration.

²⁸ With laugh, and many a kiss,
(Let others deprecate—let others weep for sin, remorse,
    humiliation ;)
O soul, thou pleasest me—I thee.

²⁹ Ah, more than any priest, O soul, we too believe in
    God ;
But with the mystery of God we dare not dally.

³⁰ O soul, thou pleasest me—I thee ;
Sailing these seas, or on the hills, or waking in the
    night,

Thoughts, silent thoughts, of Time, and Space, and
    Death, like waters flowing,
Bear me, indeed, as through the regions infinite,
Whose air I breathe, whose ripples hear—lave me all
    over :
Bathe me, O God, in thee—mounting to thee,
I and my soul to range in range of thee.

[31] O Thou transcendant !
Nameless—the fibre and the breath !
Light of the light—shedding forth universes—thou
    centre of them !
Thou mightier centre of the true, the good, the loving !
Thou moral, spiritual fountain ! affection's source ! thou
    reservoir !
(O pensive soul of me ! O thirst unsatisfied ! waitest not
    there ?
Waitest not haply for us, somewhere there, the Com-
    rade perfect ?)
Thou pulse ! thou motive of the stars, suns, systems,
That, circling, move in order, safe, harmonious,
Athwart the shapeless vastnesses of space !
How should I think—how breathe a single breath—
    how speak—if, out of myself,
I could not launch, to those, superior universes ?

[32] Swiftly I shrivel at the thought of God,
At Nature and its wonders, Time and Space and Death,
But that I, turning, call to thee, O soul, thou actual Me,
And lo ! thou gently masterest the orbs,
Thou matest Time, smilest content at Death,
And fillest, swellest full, the vastnesses of Space.

[33] Greater than stars or suns,
Bounding, O soul, thou journeyest forth ;
—What love, than thine and ours could wider amplify ?
What aspirations, wishes, outvie thine and ours, O soul ?
What dreams of the ideal ? what plans of purity, per-
    fection, strength ?

What cheerful willingness, for others' sake, to give up
all ?
For others' sake to suffer all ?

[34] Reckoning ahead, O soul, when thou, the time
achiev'd,
(The seas all cross'd, weather'd the capes, the voyage
done,)
Surrounded, copest, frontest God, yieldest, the aim
attain'd,
As, fill'd with friendship, love complete, the Elder
Brother found,
The Younger melts in fondness in his arms.

12

[35] Passage to more than India !
Are thy wings plumed indeed for such far flights ?
O Soul, voyagest thou indeed on voyages like these ?
Disportest thou on waters such as these ?
Soundest below the Sanscrit and the Vedas ?
Then have thy bent unleash'd.

[36] Passage to you, your shores, ye aged fierce enigmas !
Passage to you, to mastership of you, ye strangling
problems !
You, strew'd with the wrecks of skeletons, that, living,
never reach'd you.

13

[37] Passage to more than India !
O secret of the earth and sky !
Of you, O waters of the sea ! O winding creeks and
rivers !
Of you, O woods and fields ! Of you, strong mountains
of my land !
Of you, O prairies ! Of you, gray rocks !
O morning red ! O clouds ! O rain and snows !
O day and night, passage to you !

[38] O sun and moon, and all you stars! Sirius and
   Jupiter!
Passage to you!

[39] Passage—immediate passage! the blood burns in my
   veins!
Away, O soul! hoist instantly the anchor!
Cut the hawsers—haul out—shake out every sail!
Have we not stood here like trees in the ground long
   enough?
Have we not grovell'd here long enough, eating and
   drinking like mere brutes?
Have we not darken'd and dazed ourselves with books
   long enough?

[40] Sail forth! steer for the deep waters only!
Reckless, O soul, exploring, I with thee, and thou with
   me;
For we are bound where mariner has not yet dared to
   go,
And we will risk the ship, ourselves and all.

[41] O my brave soul!
O farther, farther sail!
O daring joy, but safe! Are they not all the seas of
   God?
O farther, farther, farther sail!

THOUGHT.

As I sit with others, at a great feast, suddenly, while
    the music is playing,
To my mind, (whence it comes I know not,) spectral, in
    mist, of a wreck at sea ;
Of certain ships—how they sail from port with flying
    streamers, and wafted kisses—and that is the
    last of them !
Of the solemn and murky mystery about the fate of the
    President ;
Of the flower of the marine science of fifty generations,
    founder'd off the Northeast coast, and going
    down—Of the steamship Arctic going down,
Of the veil'd tableau—Women gather'd together on
    deck, pale, heroic, waiting the moment that
    draws so close—O the moment !
A huge sob—A few bubbles—the white foam spirting
    up—And then the women gone,
Sinking there, while the passionless wet flows on—And
    I now pondering, Are those women indeed gone ?
Are Souls drown'd and destroy'd so ?
Is only matter triumphant ?

O LIVING ALWAYS—ALWAYS DYING !

O living always—always dying !
O the burials of me, past and present !
O me, while I stride ahead, material, visible, imperious
    as ever !
O me, what I was for years, now dead, (I lament not—
    I am content ;)
O to disengage myself from those corpses of me, which
    I turn and look at, where I cast them !
To pass on, (O living ! always living !) and leave the
    corpses behind !

Proud Music of the Storm.

——◦◦◦——

1

[1] Proud music of the storm!
Blast that careers so free, whistling across the prairies!
Strong hum of forest tree-tops! Wind of the moun-
    tains!
Personified dim shapes! you hidden orchestras!
You serenades of phantoms, with instruments alert,
Blending, with Nature's rhythmus, all the tongues of
    nations;
You chords left as by vast composers! you choruses!
You formless, free, religious dances! you from the
    Orient!
You undertone of rivers, roar of pouring cataracts;
You sounds from distant guns, with galloping cavalry!
Echoes of camps, with all the different bugle-calls!
Trooping tumultuous, filling the midnight late, bending
    me powerless,
Entering my lonesome slumber-chamber—Why have
    you seiz'd me?

2

[2] Come forward, O my Soul, and let the rest retire;
Listen—lose not—it is toward thee they tend;
Parting the midnight, entering my slumber-chamber,
For thee they sing and dance, O Soul.

² A festival song!
The duet of the bridegroom and the bride—a marriage-
      march,
With lips of love, and hearts of lovers, fill'd to the brim
      with love ;
The red-flush'd cheeks, and perfumes — the cortege
      swarming, full of friendly faces, young and old,
To flutes' clear notes, and sounding harps' cantabile.

3

⁴ Now loud approaching drums!
Victoria! see'st thou in powder-smoke the banners torn
      but flying? the rout of the baffled?
Hearest those shouts of a conquering army?

⁵ (Ah, Soul, the sobs of women—the wounded groaning
      in agony,
The hiss and crackle of flames—the blacken'd ruins—
      the embers of cities,
The dirge and desolation of mankind.)

4

⁶ Now airs antique and medieval fill me!
I see and hear old harpers with their harps, at Welsh
      festivals :
I hear the minnesingers, singing their lays of love,
I hear the minstrels, gleemen, troubadours, of the feudal
      ages.

5

⁷ Now the great organ sounds,
Tremulous—while underneath, (as the hid footholds of
      the earth,
On which arising, rest, and leaping forth, depend,
All shapes of beauty, grace and strength—all hues we
      know,
Green blades of grass, and warbling birds—children
      that gambol and play—the clouds of heaven
      above,)

The strong base stands, and its pulsations intermits
    not,
Bathing, supporting, merging all the rest—maternity
    of all the rest ;
And with it every instrument in multitudes,
The players playing—all the world's musicians,
The solemn hymns and masses, rousing adoration,
All passionate heart-chants, sorrowful appeals,
The measureless sweet vocalists of ages,
And for their solvent setting, Earth's own diapason,
Of winds and woods and mighty ocean waves ;
A new composite orchestra—binder of years and climes
    —ten-fold renewer,
As of the far-back days the poets tell—the Paradiso,
The straying thence, the separation long, but now the
    wandering done,
The journey done, the Journeyman come home,
And Man and Art with Nature fused again.

6

[8] Tutti ! for Earth and Heaven !
The Almighty Leader now for me, for once, has signal'd
    with his wand.

[9] The manly strophe of the husbands of the world,
And all the wives responding.

[10] The tongues of violins !
(I think, O tongues, ye tell this heart, that cannot tell
    itself ;
This brooding, yearning heart, that cannot tell itself.)

7

[11] Ah, from a little child,
Thou knowest, Soul, how to me all sounds became
    music ;
My mother's voice, in lullaby or hymn ;
(The voice—O tender voices—memory's loving voices !
Last miracle of all—O dearest mother's, sister's, voices:)

The rain, the growing corn, the breeze among the
    long-leav'd corn,
The measur'd sea-surf, beating on the sand,
The twittering bird, the hawk's sharp scream,
The wild-fowl's notes at night, as flying low, migrating
    north or south,
The psalm in the country church, or mid the clustering
    trees, the open air camp-meeting,
The fiddler in the tavern—the glee, the long-strung
    sailor-song,
The lowing cattle, bleating sheep—the crowing cock at
    dawn.

8

[12] All songs of current lands come sounding 'round me,
The German airs of friendship, wine and love,
Irish ballads, merry jigs and dances—English warbles,
Chansons of France, Scotch tunes—and o'er the rest,
Italia's peerless compositions.

[13] Across the stage, with pallor on her face, yet lurid
    passion,
Stalks Norma, brandishing the dagger in her hand.

[14] I see poor crazed Lucia's eyes' unnatural gleam ;
Her hair down her back falls loose and dishevell'd.

[15] I see where Ernani, walking the bridal garden,
Amid the scent of night-roses, radiant, holding his
    bride by the hand,
Hears the infernal call, the death-pledge of the horn.

[16] To crossing swords, and grey hairs bared to heaven,
The clear, electric base and baritone of the world,
The trombone duo—Libertad forever !

[17] From Spanish chestnut trees' dense shade,
By old and heavy convent walls, a wailing song,
Song of lost love—the torch of youth and life quench'd
    in despair,
Song of the dying swan—Fernando's heart is breaking.

[18] Awaking from her woes at last, retriev'd Amina
          sings ;
Copious as stars, and glad as morning light, the tor-
          rents of her joy.

[19] (The teeming lady comes !
The   lustrous   orb—Venus   contralto—the   blooming
          mother,
Sister of loftiest gods—Alboni's self I hear.)

9

[20] I hear those odes, symphonies, operas ;
I hear in the *William Tell*, the music of an arous'd and
          angry people ;
I hear Meyerbeer's *Huguenots*, the *Prophet*, or *Robert ;*
Gounod's *Faust*, or Mozart's *Don Juan.*

10

[21] I hear the dance-music of all nations,
The waltz, (some delicious measure, lapsing, bathing me
          in bliss ;)
The bolero, to tinkling guitars and clattering castanets.

[22] I see religious dances old and new,
I hear the sound of the Hebrew lyre,
I see the Crusaders marching, bearing the cross on
          high, to the martial clang of cymbals ;
I hear dervishes monotonously chanting, interspers'd
          with frantic shouts, as they spin around, turning
          always towards Mecca ;
I see the rapt religious dances of the Persians and the
          Arabs ;
Again, at Eleusis, home of Ceres, I see the modern
          Greeks dancing,
I hear them clapping their hands, as they bend their
          bodies,
I hear the metrical shuffling of their feet.

[23] I see again the wild old Corybantian dance, the per-
    formers wounding each other ;
I see the Roman youth, to the shrill sound of flageolets,
    throwing and catching their weapons,
As they fall on their knees, and rise again.

[24] I hear from the Mussulman mosque the muezzin
    calling ;
I see the worshippers within, (nor form, nor sermon,
    argument, nor word,
But silent, strange, devout—rais'd, glowing heads—
    extatic faces.)

11

[25] I hear the Egyptian harp of many strings,
The primitive chants of the Nile boatmen ;
The sacred imperial hymns of China,
To the delicate sounds of the king, (the stricken wood
    and stone ;)
Or to Hindu flutes, and the fretting twang of the vina,
A band of bayaderes.

12

[26] Now Asia, Africa leave me—Europe, seizing, inflates
    me ;
To organs huge, and bands, I hear as from vast con-
    courses of voices,
Luther's strong hymn, *Eine feste Burg ist unser Gott ;*
Rossini's *Stabat Mater dolorosa ;*
Or, floating in some high cathedral dim, with gorgeous
    color'd windows,
The passionate *Agnus Dei,* or *Gloria in Excelsis.*

13

[27] Composers ! mighty maestros !
And you, sweet singers of old lands—Soprani ! Tenori !
    Bassi !
To you a new bard, carolling free in the west,
Obeisant, sends his love.

[28] (Such led to thee, O Soul!
All senses, shows and objects, lead to thee,
But now, it seems to me, sound leads o'er all the
    rest.)

14

[29] I hear the annual singing of the children in St. Paul's
    Cathedral ;
Or, under the high roof of some colossal hall, the sym-
    phonies, oratorios of Beethoven, Handel, or
    Haydn ;
The *Creation*, in billows of godhood laves me.

[30] Give me to hold all sounds, (I, madly struggling,
    cry,)
Fill me with all the voices of the universe,
Endow me with their throbbings—Nature's also,
The tempests, waters, winds—operas and chants—
    marches and dances,
Utter—pour in—for I would take them all.

15

[31] Then I woke softly,
And pausing, questioning awhile the music of my
    dream,
And questioning all those reminiscences—the tempest
    in its fury,
And all the songs of sopranos and tenors,
And those rapt oriental dances, of religious fervor,
And the sweet varied instruments, and the diapason of
    organs,
And all the artless plaints of love, and grief and
    death,
I said to my silent, curious Soul, out of the bed of the
    slumber-chamber,
Come, for I have found the clue I sought so long,
Let us go forth refresh'd amid the day,
Cheerfully tallying life, walking the world, the real,
Nourish'd henceforth by our celestial dream.

[32] And I said, moreover,
Haply, what thou hast heard, O Soul, was not the sound
    of winds,
Nor dream of raging storm, nor sea-hawk's flapping
    wings, nor harsh scream,
Nor vocalism of sun-bright Italy,
Nor German organ majestic—nor vast concourse of
    voices—nor layers of harmonies ;
Nor strophes of husbands and wives—nor sound of
    marching soldiers,
Nor flutes, nor harps, nor the bugle-calls of camps ;
But, to a new rhythmus fitted for thee,
Poems, bridging the way from Life to Death, vaguely
    wafted in night air, uncaught, unwritten,
Which, let us go forth in the bold day, and write.

ASHES OF SOLDIERS.

Again a verse for sake of you,
You soldiers in the ranks—you Volunteers,
Who bravely fighting, silent fell,
To fill unmention'd graves.

ASHES OF SOLDIERS.

[1] Ashes of soldiers !
As I muse, retrospective, murmuring a chant in thought,
Lo! the war resumes—again to my sense your shapes,
And again the advance of armies.

[2] Noiseless as mists and vapors,
From their graves in the trenches ascending,
From the cemeteries all through Virginia and Ten-
nessee,
From every point of the compass, out of the countless
unnamed graves,
In wafted clouds, in myriads large, or squads of twos
or threes, or single ones, they come,
And silently gather round me,

[3] Now sound no note, O trumpeters !
Not at the head of my cavalry, parading on spirited
horses,
With sabres drawn and glist'ning, and carbines by
their thighs—(ah, my brave horsemen !

2

My handsome, tan-faced horsemen! what life, what joy
  and pride,
With all the perils, were yours!)

4 Nor you drummers—neither at reveille, at dawn,
Nor the long roll alarming the camp—nor even the
  muffled beat for a burial;
Nothing from you, this time, O drummers, bearing my
  warlike drums.

5 But aside from these, and the marts of wealth, and
  the crowded promenade,
Admitting around me comrades close, unseen by the
  rest, and voiceless,
The slain elate and alive again—the dust and debris
  alive,
I chant this chant of my silent soul, in the name of all
  dead soldiers.

6 Faces so pale, with wondrous eyes, very dear, gather
  closer yet;
Draw close, but speak not.

7 Phantoms of countless lost!
Invisible to the rest, henceforth become my compan-
  ions!
Follow me ever! desert me not, while I live.

8 Sweet are the blooming cheeks of the living! sweet
  are the musical voices sounding!
But sweet, ah sweet, are the dead, with their silent eyes.

9 Dearest comrades! all is over and long gone;
But love is not over—and what love, O comrades!
Perfume from battle-fields rising — up from fœtor
  arising.

10 Perfume therefore my chant, O love! immortal Love!
Give me to bathe the memories of all dead soldiers,
Shroud them, embalm them, cover them all over with
  tender pride.

[11] Perfume all! make all wholesome!
Make these ashes to nourish and blossom,
O love! O chant! solve all, fructify all with the last
    chemistry.

[12] Give me exhaustless—make me a fountain,
That I exhale love from me wherever I go, like a moist
    perennial dew,
For the ashes of all dead soldiers.

IN MIDNIGHT SLEEP.

1

In midnight sleep, of many a face of anguish,
Of the look at first of the mortally wounded—of that
    indescribable look;
Of the dead on their backs, with arms extended wide,
    I dream, I dream, I dream.

2

Of scenes of nature, fields and mountains;
Of skies, so beauteous after a storm—and at night the
    moon so unearthly bright,
Shining sweetly, shining down, where we dig the
    trenches and gather the heaps,
    I dream, I dream, I dream.

3

Long, long have they pass'd—faces and trenches and
    fields;
Where through the carnage I moved with a callous com-
    posure—or away from the fallen,
Onward I sped at the time—But now of their forms at
    night,
    I dream, I dream, I dream.

CAMPS OF GREEN.

[1] NOT alone those camps of white, O soldiers,
When, as order'd forward, after a long march,
Footsore and weary, soon as the light lessen'd, we
      halted for the night ;
Some of us so fatigued, carrying the gun and knapsack,
      dropping asleep in our tracks ;
Others pitching the little tents, and the fires lit up
      began to sparkle ;
Outposts of pickets posted, surrounding, alert through
      the dark,
And a word provided for countersign, careful for safety;
Till to the call of the drummers at daybreak loudly
      beating the drums,
We rose up refresh'd, the night and sleep pass'd over,
      and resumed our journey,
Or proceeded to battle.

[2] Lo! the camps of the tents of green,
Which the days of peace keep filling, and the days of
      war keep filling,
With a mystic army, (is it too order'd forward ? is it
      too only halting awhile,
Till night and sleep pass over ?)

[3] Now in those camps of green—in their tents dotting
      the world ;
In the parents, children, husbands, wives, in them—in
      the old and young,
Sleeping under the sunlight, sleeping under the moon-
      light, content and silent there at last,
Behold the mighty bivouac-field, and waiting-camp of
      all,
Of corps and generals all, and the President over the
      corps and generals all,
And of each of us, O soldiers, and of each and all in
      the ranks we fought,
(There without hatred we shall all meet.)

' For presently, O soldiers, we too camp in our place in
    the bivouac-camps of green ;
But we need not provide for outposts, nor word for the
    countersign,
Nor drummer to beat the morning drum.

TO A CERTAIN CIVILIAN.

DID YOU ask dulcet rhymes from me?
Did you seek the civilian's peaceful and languishing
    rhymes?
Did you find what I sang erewhile so hard to follow?
Why I was not singing erewhile for you to follow, to
    understand—nor am I now ;
(I have been born of the same as the war was born ;
The drum-corps' harsh rattle is to me sweet music—I
    love well the martial dirge,
With slow wail, and convulsive throb, leading the offi-
    cer's funeral :)
—What to such as you, anyhow, such a poet as I ?—
    therefore leave my works,
And go lull yourself with what you can understand—
    and with piano-tunes ;
For I lull nobody—and you will never understand me.

PENSIVE ON HER DEAD GAZING, I HEARD THE
MOTHER OF ALL.

PENSIVE, on her dead gazing, I heard the Mother of All,
Desperate, on the torn bodies, on the forms covering
    the battle-fields gazing ;
(As the last gun ceased—but the scent of the powder-
    smoke linger'd ;)
As she call'd to her earth with mournful voice while she
    stalk'd :

Absorb them well, O my earth, she cried—I charge you,
   lose not my sons! lose not an atom ;
And you streams, absorb them well, taking their dear
   blood ;
And you local spots, and you airs that swim above
   lightly,
And all you essences of soil and growth—and you, my
   rivers' depths ;
And you, mountain sides—and the woods where my
   dear children's blood, trickling, redden'd ;
And you trees, down in your roots, to bequeath to all
   future trees,
My dead absorb—my young men's beautiful bodies
   absorb—and their precious, precious, precious
   blood ;
Which holding in trust for me, faithfully back again
   give me, many a year hence,
In unseen essence and odor of surface and grass, centuries hence ;
In blowing airs from the fields, back again give me my
   darlings—give my immortal heroes ;
Exhale me them centuries hence—breathe me their
   breath—let not an atom be lost ;
O years and graves! O air and soil! O my dead, an
   aroma sweet !
Exhale them perennial, sweet death, years, centuries
   hence.

President Lincoln's Burial Hymn.

—

WHEN LILACS LAST IN THE DOOR-YARD BLOOM'D.

1

[1] WHEN lilacs last in the door-yard bloom'd,
And the great star early droop'd in the western sky in
    the night,
I mourn'd—and yet shall mourn with ever-returning
    spring.

[2] O ever-returning spring! trinity sure to me you
    bring ;
Lilac blooming perennial, and drooping star in the
    west,
And thought of him I love.

2

[3] O powerful, western, fallen star!
O shades of night! O moody, tearful night!
O great star disappear'd! O the black murk that hides
    the star!
O cruel hands that hold me powerless! O helpless soul
    of me!
O harsh surrounding cloud, that will not free my soul!

3

[4] In the door-yard fronting an old farm-house, near the
    white-wash'd palings,
Stands the lilac bush, tall-growing, with heart-shaped
    leaves of rich green,
With many a pointed blossom, rising, delicate, with the
    perfume strong I love,
With every leaf a miracle ...... and from this bush in
    the door-yard,
With delicate-color'd blossoms, and heart-shaped leaves
    of rich green,
A sprig, with its flower, I break.

4

[5] In the swamp, in secluded recesses,
A shy and hidden bird is warbling a song.

[6] Solitary, the thrush,
The hermit, withdrawn to himself, avoiding the settle-
    ments,
Sings by himself a song.

[7] Song of the bleeding throat!
Death's outlet song of life—(for well, dear brother, I
    know,
If thou wast not gifted to sing, thou would'st surely
    die.)

5

[8] Over the breast of the spring, the land, amid cities,
Amid lanes, and through old woods, (where lately the
    violets peep'd from the ground, spotting the gray
    debris ;)
Amid the grass in the fields each side of the lanes—
    passing the endless grass ;
Passing the yellow-spear'd wheat, every grain from its
    shroud in the dark-brown fields uprising ;
Passing the apple-tree blows of white and pink in the
    orchards :

Carrying a corpse to where it shall rest in the grave,
Night and day journeys a coffin.

6

[9] Coffin that passes through lanes and streets,
Through day and night, with the great cloud darkening
    the land,
With the pomp of the inloop'd flags, with the cities
    draped in black,
With the show of the States themselves, as of crape-
    veil'd women, standing,
With processions long and winding, and the flambeaus
    of the night,
With the countless torches lit—with the silent sea of
    faces, and the unbared heads,
With the waiting depot, the arriving coffin, and the
    sombre faces,
With dirges through the night, with the thousand voices
    rising strong and solemn ;
With all the mournful voices of the dirges. pour'd around
    the coffin,
The dim-lit churches and the shuddering organs—Where
    amid these you journey,
With the tolling, tolling bells' perpetual clang ;
Here ! coffin that slowly passes,
I give you my sprig of lilac.

7

[10] (Nor for you, for one, alone ;
Blossoms and branches green to coffins all I bring :
For fresh as the morning—thus would I carol a song
    for you, O sane and sacred death.

[11] All over bouquets of roses,
O death ! I cover you over with roses and early lilies ;
But mostly and now the lilac that blooms the first,
Copious, I break, I break the sprigs from the bushes ;
With loaded arms I come, pouring for you,
For you, and the coffins all of you, O death.)

8

[12] O western orb, sailing the heaven!
Now I know what you must have meant, as a month
    since we walk'd,
As we walk'd up and down in the dark blue so mystic,
As we walk'd in silence the transparent shadowy night,
As I saw you had something to tell, as you bent to me
    night after night,
As you droop'd from the sky low down, as if to my side,
    (while the other stars all look'd on ;)
As we wander'd together the solemn night, (for some-
    thing, I know not what, kept me from sleep ;)
As the night advanced, and I saw on the rim of the
    west, ere you went, how full you were of woe ;
As I stood on the rising ground in the breeze, in the
    cold transparent night,
As I watch'd where you pass'd and was lost in the
    netherward black of the night,
As my soul, in its trouble, dissatisfied, sank, as where
    you, sad orb,
Concluded, dropt in the night, and was gone.

9

[13] Sing on, there in the swamp!
O singer bashful and tender! I hear your notes—I hear
    your call ;
I hear—I come presently—I understand you ;
But a moment I linger—for the lustrous star has de-
    tain'd me ;
The star, my departing comrade, holds and detains me.

10

[14] O how shall I warble myself for the dead one there I
    loved ?
And how shall I deck my song for the large sweet soul
    that has gone ?
And what shall my perfume be, for the grave of him I
    love ?

[15] Sea-winds, blown from east and west,
Blown from the eastern sea, and blown from the west-
　　ern sea, till there on the prairies meeting:
These, and with these, and the breath of my chant,
I perfume the grave of him I love.

11

[16] O what shall I hang on the chamber walls?
And what shall the pictures be that I hang on the
　　walls,
To adorn the burial-house of him I love?

[17] Pictures of growing spring, and farms, and homes,
With the Fourth-month eve at sundown, and the gray
　　smoke lucid and bright,
With floods of the yellow gold of the gorgeous, indo-
　　lent, sinking sun, burning, expanding the air;
With the fresh sweet herbage under foot, and the pale
　　green leaves of the trees prolific;
In the distance the flowing glaze, the breast of the river,
　　with a wind-dapple here and there;
With ranging hills on the banks, with many a line
　　against the sky, and shadows;
And the city at hand, with dwellings so dense, and
　　stacks of chimneys,
And all the scenes of life, and the workshops, and the
　　workmen homeward returning.

12

[18] Lo! body and soul! this land!
Mighty Manhattan, with spires, and the sparkling and
　　hurrying tides, and the ships;
The varied and ample land—the South and the North
　　in the light—Ohio's shores, and flashing Mis-
　　souri,
And ever the far-spreading prairies, cover'd with grass
　　and corn.

[19] Lo! the most excellent sun, so calm and haughty;
The violet and purple morn, with just-felt breezes;

The gentle, soft-born, measureless light ;
The miracle, spreading, bathing all — the fulfill'd
     noon ;
The coming eve, delicious—the welcome night, and the
     stars,
Over my cities shining all, enveloping man and land.

13

[20] Sing on ! sing on, you gray-brown bird !
Sing from the swamps, the recesses—pour your chant
     from the bushes ;
Limitless out of the dusk, out of the cedars and
     pines.

[21] Sing on, dearest brother—warble your reedy song ;
Loud human song, with voice of uttermost woe.

[22] O liquid, and free, and tender !
O wild and loose to my soul ! O wondrous singer !
You only I hear . . . . . . yet the star holds me, (but will
     soon depart ;)
Yet the lilac, with mastering odor, holds me.

14

[23] Now while I sat in the day, and look'd forth,
In the close of the day, with its light, and the fields of
     spring, and the farmer preparing his crops,
In the large unconscious scenery of my land, with its
     lakes and forests,
In the heavenly aerial beauty, (after the perturb'd
     winds, and the storms ;)
Under the arching heavens of the afternoon swift pass-
     ing, and the voices of children and women,
The many-moving sea-tides,—and I saw the ships how
     they sail'd,
And the summer approaching with richness, and the
     fields all busy with labor,
And the infinite separate houses, how they all went on,
     each with its meals and minutia of daily usages ;

And the streets, how their throbbings throbb'd, and the
　　cities pent—lo ! then and there,
Falling upon them all, and among them all, enveloping
　　me with the rest,
Appear'd the cloud, appear'd the long black trail ;
And I knew Death, its thought, and the sacred knowl-
　　edge of death.

15

[24] Then with the knowledge of death as walking one
　　side of me,
And the thought of death close-walking the other side
　　of me,
And I in the middle, as with companions, and as hold-
　　ing the hands of companions,
I fled forth to the hiding receiving night, that talks
　　not,
Down to the shores of the water, the path by the swamp
　　in the dimness,
To the solemn shadowy cedars, and ghostly pines so
　　still.

[25] And the singer so shy to the rest receiv'd me ;
The gray-brown bird I know, receiv'd us comrades
　　three ;
And he sang what seem'd the carol of death, and a
　　verse for him I love.

[26] From deep secluded recesses,
From the fragrant cedars, and the ghostly pines so
　　still,
Came the carol of the bird.

[27] And the charm of the carol rapt me,
As I held, as if by their hands, my comrades in the
　　night ;
And the voice of my spirit tallied the song of the
　　bird.

DEATH CAROL.

16

[28] *Come, lovely and soothing Death,*
Undulate round the world, serenely arriving, arriving,
In the day, in the night, to all, to each,
Sooner or later, delicate Death.

[29] *Prais'd be the fathomless universe,*
For life and joy, and for objects and knowledge curious ;
And for love, sweet love—But praise ! praise ! praise !
For the sure-enwinding arms of cool-enfolding Death.

[30] *Dark Mother, always gliding near, with soft feet,*
Have none chanted for thee a chant of fullest welcome ?
Then I chant it for thee—I glorify thee above all ;
I bring thee a song that when thou must indeed come, come
  unfalteringly.

[31] *Approach, strong Deliveress !*
When it is so—when thou hast taken them, I joyously sing
  the dead,
Lost in the loving, floating ocean of thee,
Laved in the flood of thy bliss, O Death.

[32] *From me to thee glad serenades,*
Dances for thee I propose, saluting thee—adornments and
  feastings for thee ;
And the sights of the open landscape, and the high-spread
  sky, are fitting,
And life and the fields, and the huge and thoughtful night.

[33] *The night, in silence, under many a star ;*
The ocean shore, and the husky whispering wave, whose
  voice I know ;
And the soul turning to thee, O vast and well-veil'd Death,
And the body gratefully nestling close to thee.

[34] *Over the tree-tops I float thee a song !*
Over the rising and sinking waves—over the myriad fields,
  and the prairies wide ;

*Over the dense-pack'd cities all, and the teeming wharves
        and ways,
I float this carol with joy, with joy to thee, O Death !*

17

[35] To the tally of my soul,
Loud and strong kept up the gray-brown bird,
With pure, deliberate notes, spreading, filling the night.

[26] Loud in the pines and cedars dim,
Clear in the freshness moist, and the swamp-perfume ;
And I with my comrades there in the night.

[37] While my sight that was bound in my eyes unclosed,
As to long panoramas of visions.

18

[28] I saw askant the armies ;
And I saw, as in noiseless dreams, hundreds of battle-
        flags ;
Borne through the smoke of the battles, and pierc'd
        with missiles, I saw them,
And carried hither and yon through the smoke, and
        torn and bloody ;
And at last but a few shreds left on the staffs, (and all
        in silence,)
And the staffs all splinter'd and broken.

[39] I saw battle-corpses, myriads of them,
And the white skeletons of young men—I saw them ;
I saw the debris and debris of all the dead soldiers of
        the war ;
But I saw they were not as was thought ;
They themselves were fully at rest—they suffer'd not ;
The living remain'd and suffer'd—the mother suffer'd,
And the wife and the child, and the musing comrade
        suffer'd,
And the armies that remain'd suffer'd.

19

[40] Passing the visions, passing the night ;
Passing, unloosing the hold of my comrades' hands ;

Passing the song of the hermit bird, and the tallying
    song of my soul,
(Victorious song, death's outlet song, yet varying, ever-
    altering song,
As low and wailing, yet clear the notes, rising and fall-
    ing, flooding the night,
Sadly sinking and fainting, as warning and warning,
    and yet again bursting with joy,
Covering the earth, and filling the spread of the heaven,
As that powerful psalm in the night I heard from
    recesses,)
Passing, I leave thee, lilac with heart-shaped leaves;
I leave thee there in the door-yard, blooming, returning
    with spring.

[41] I cease from my song for thee;
From my gaze on thee in the west, fronting the west,
    communing with thee,
O comrade lustrous, with silver face in the night.

20

[42] Yet each I keep, and all, retrievements out of the
    night;
The song, the wondrous chant of the gray-brown bird,
And the tallying chant, the echo arous'd in my soul,
With the lustrous and drooping star, with the counte-
    nance full of woe,
With the lilac tall, and its blossoms of mastering odor;
With the holders holding my hand, nearing the call of
    the bird,
Comrades mine, and I in the midst, and their memory
    ever I keep—for the dead I loved so well;
For the sweetest, wisest soul of all my days and lands...
    and this for his dear sake;
Lilac and star and bird, twined with the chant of my
    soul,
There in the fragrant pines, and the cedars dusk and dim.

O CAPTAIN! MY CAPTAIN!

1

O CAPTAIN! my Captain! our fearful trip is done;
The ship has weather'd every rack, the prize we sought
    is won;
The port is near, the bells I hear, the people all exulting,
While follow eyes the steady keel, the vessel grim and
    daring:
    But O heart! heart! heart!
      O the bleeding drops of red,
        Where on the deck my Captain lies,
        Fallen cold and dead.

2

O Captain! my Captain! rise up and hear the bells;
Rise up—for you the flag is flung—for you the bugle
    trills;
For you bouquets and ribbon'd wreaths—for you the
    shores a-crowding;
For you they call, the swaying mass, their eager faces
    turning;
    Here Captain! dear father!
      This arm beneath your head;
        It is some dream that on the deck,
        You've fallen cold and dead.

3

My Captain does not answer, his lips are pale and still;
My father does not feel my arm, he has no pulse nor will;
The ship is anchor'd safe and sound, its voyage closed
    and done;
From fearful trip, the victor ship, comes in with object
    won:
    Exult, O shores, and ring, O bells!
      But I, with mournful tread,
        Walk the deck my Captain lies,
        Fallen cold and dead.

HUSH'D BE THE CAMPS TO-DAY.

(*May* 4, 1865)

1

Hush'd be the camps to day ;
And, soldiers, let us drape our war-worn weapons ;
And each with musing soul retire, to celebrate,
Our dear commander's death.

2 No more for him life's stormy conflicts ;
Nor victory, nor defeat—no more time's dark events,
Charging like ceaseless clouds across the sky.

2

3 But sing, poet, in our name ;
Sing of the love we bore him—because you, dweller in
    camps, know it truly.

4 As they invault the coffin there ;
Sing—as they close the doors of earth upon him—
    one verse,
For the heavy hearts of soldiers.

THIS DUST WAS ONCE THE MAN.

This dust was once the Man,
Gentle, plain, just and resolute—under whose cautious
    hand,
Against the foulest crime in history known in any land
    or age,
Was saved the Union of These States.

POEM OF JOYS.

1

[1] O to make the most jubilant poem!
Even to set off these, and merge with these, the carols
    of Death;
O full of music! full of manhood, womanhood, in-
    fancy!
Full of common employments! full of grain and trees.

[2] O for the voices of animals! O for the swiftness and
    balance of fishes!
O for the dropping of rain-drops in a poem!
O for the sunshine, and motion of waves in a poem.

[3] O the joy of my spirit! it is uncaged! it darts like
    lightning!
It is not enough to have this globe, or a certain time—
    I will have thousands of globes, and all time.

2

[4] O the engineer's joys!
To go with a locomotive!
To hear the hiss of steam—the merry shriek—the
    steam-whistle—the laughing locomotive!
To push with resistless way, and speed off in the dis-
    tance.

[5] O the gleesome saunter over fields and hill-sides!

The leaves and flowers of the commonest weeds—the
    moist fresh stillness of the woods,
The exquisite smell of the earth at day-break, and
    all through the forenoon.

6 O the horseman's and horsewoman's joys!
The saddle—the gallop—the pressure upon the seat—
    the cool gurgling by the ears and hair.

3

7 O the fireman's joys!
I hear the alarm at dead of night,
I hear bells—shouts!—I pass the crowd—I run!
The sight of the flames maddens me with pleasure.

8 O the joy of the strong-brawn'd fighter, towering in
    the arena, in perfect condition, conscious of
    power, thirsting to meet his opponent.

9 O the joy of that vast elemental sympathy which only
    the human Soul is capable of generating and
    emitting in steady and limitless floods.

4

10 O the mother's joys!
The watching—the endurance—the precious love—the
    anguish—the patiently yielded life.

11 O the joy of increase, growth, recuperation;
The joy of soothing and pacifying—the joy of concord
    and harmony.

12 O to go back to the place where I was born!
To hear the birds sing once more!
To ramble about the house and barn, and over the
    fields, once more,
And through the orchard and along the old lanes once
    more.

5

13 O male and female!

O the presence of women! (I swear there is nothing
　　more exquisite to me than the mere presence of
　　women ;)
O for the girl, my mate! O for the happiness with my
　　mate!
O the young man as I pass! O I am sick after the
　　friendship of him who, I fear, is indifferent to
　　me.

[14] O the streets of cities!
The flitting faces—the expressions, eyes, feet, costumes!
　　O I cannot tell how welcome they are to me.

6

[15] O to have been brought up on bays, lagoons, creeks,
　　or along the coast!
O to continue and be employ'd there all my life!
O the briny and damp smell—the shore—the salt weeds
　　exposed at low water,
The work of fishermen—the work of the eel-fisher and
　　clam-fisher.

[16] O it is I!
I come with my clam-rake and spade! I come with my
　　eel-spear ;
Is the tide out? I join the group of clam-diggers on the
　　flats,
I laugh and work with them—I joke at my work, like a
　　mettlesome young man.

[17] In winter I take my eel-basket and eel-spear and
　　travel out on foot on the ice—I have a small axe
　　to cut holes in the ice ;
Behold me, well-clothed, going gaily, or returning in
　　the afternoon—my brood of tough boys accom-
　　panying me,
My brood of grown and part-grown boys, who love to
　　be with no one else so well as they love to be
　　with me,
By day to work with me, and by night to sleep with me.

[18] Or, another time, in warm weather, out in a boat, to
       lift the lobster-pots, where they are sunk with
       heavy stones, (I know the buoys ;)
O the sweetness of the Fifth-month morning upon the
       water, as I row, just before sunrise, toward the
       buoys ;
I pull the wicker pots up slantingly—the dark green
       lobsters are desperate with their claws, as I take
       them out—I insert wooden pegs in the joints of
       their pincers,
I go to all the places, one after another, and then row
       back to the shore,
There, in a huge kettle of boiling water, the lobsters
       shall be boil'd till their color becomes scarlet.

[19] Or, another time, mackerel-taking,
Voracious, mad for the hook, near the surface, they
       seem to fill the water for miles:
Or, another time, fishing for rock-fish in Chesapeake
       Bay—I one of the brown-faced crew :
Or, another time, trailing for blue-fish off Paumanok, I
       stand with braced body,
My left foot is on the gunwale—my right arm throws
       the coils of slender rope,
In sight around me the quick veering and darting of
       fifty skiffs, my companions.

7

[20] O boating on the rivers !
The voyage down the Niagara, (the St. Lawrence,)—
       the superb scenery—the steamers,
The ships sailing—the Thousand Islands—the occa-
       sional timber-raft, and the raftsmen with long-
       reaching sweep-oars,
The little huts on the rafts, and the stream of smoke
       when they cook supper at evening.

[21] O something pernicious and dread !
Something far away from a puny and pious life !
Something unproved ! Something in a trance !

Something escaped from the anchorage, and driving
free.

[22] O to work in mines, or forging iron!
Foundry casting—the foundry itself—the rude high
roof—the ample and shadow'd space,
The furnace—the hot liquid pour'd out and running.

8

[23] O to resume the joys of the soldier:
To feel the presence of a brave general! to feel his sym-
pathy!
To behold his calmness! to be warm'd in the rays of his
smile!
To go to battle! to hear the bugles play, and the drums
beat!
To hear the crash of artillery! to see the glittering of
the bayonets and musket-barrels in the sun!
To see men fall and die, and not complain!
To taste the savage taste of blood! to be so devilish!
To gloat so over the wounds and deaths of the enemy.

9

[24] O the whaleman's joys! O I cruise my old cruise
again!
I feel the ship's motion under me—I feel the Atlantic
breezes fanning me,
I hear the cry again sent down from the mast-head—
There—she blows!
—Again I spring up the rigging, to look with the rest
—We see—we descend, wild with excitement,
I leap in the lower'd boat—We row toward our prey,
where he lies,
We approach, stealthy and silent—I see the mountain-
ous mass, lethargic, basking,
I see the harpooneer standing up—I see the weapon
dart from his vigorous arm:
O swift, again, now, far out in the ocean, the wounded
whale, settling, running to windward, tows me;

—Again I see him rise to breathe—We row close
 again,
I see a lance driven through his side, press'd deep,
 turn'd in the wound,
Again we back off—I see him settle again—the life is
 leaving him fast,
As he rises, he spouts blood—I see him swim in circles
 narrower and narrower, swiftly cutting the water
 —I see him die ;
He gives one convulsive leap in the centre of the circle,
 and then falls flat and still in the bloody foam.

10

²⁵ O the old manhood of me, my joy!
My children and grand-children—my white hair and
 beard,
My largeness, calmness, majesty, out of the long stretch
 of my life.

²⁶ O the ripen'd joy of womanhood!
O perfect happiness at last!
I am more than eighty years of age—my hair, too, is
 pure white—I am the most venerable mother ;
How clear is my mind! how all people draw nigh to
 me!
What attractions are these, beyond any before? what
 bloom, more than the bloom of youth?
What beauty is this that descends upon me, and rises
 out of me?

²⁷ O the orator's joys!
To inflate the chest—to roll the thunder of the voice
 out from the ribs and throat,
To make the people rage, weep, hate, desire, with your-
 self,
To lead America—to quell America with a great tongue.

²⁸ O the joy of my soul leaning pois'd on itself—receiving identity through materials, and loving them
 —observing characters, and absorbing them ;

O my soul, vibrated back to me, from them—from
    facts, sight, hearing, touch, my phrenology,
    reason, articulation, comparison, memory, and
    the like ;
The real life of my senses and flesh, transcending my
    senses and flesh ;
My body, done with materials—my sight, done with
    my material eyes ;
Proved to me this day, beyond cavil, that it is not my
    material eyes which finally see,
Nor my material body which finally loves, walks, laughs,
    shouts, embraces, procreates.

11

[29] O the farmer's joys!
Ohioan's, Illinoisian's, Wisconsinese', Kanadian's, Io-
    wan's, Kansian's, Missourian's, Oregonese' joys ;
To rise at peep of day, and pass forth nimbly to work,
To plow land in the fall for winter-sown crops,
To plough land in the spring for maize,
To train orchards—to graft the trees—to gather apples
    in the fall.

[30] O the pleasure with trees !
The orchard—the forest—the oak, cedar, pine, pekan-
    tree,
The honey-locust, black-walnut, cottonwood, and mag-
    nolia.

12

[31] O Death ! the voyage of Death !
The beautiful touch of Death, soothing and benumbing
    a few moments, for reasons ;
Myself, discharging my excrementitious body, to be
    burn'd, or render'd to powder, or buried,
My real body doubtless left to me for other spheres,
My voided body, nothing more to me, returning to the
    purifications, further offices, eternal uses of the
    earth.

13

[32] O to bathe in the swimming-bath, or in a good place
      along shore !
To splash the water ! to walk ankle-deep—to race naked
      along the shore.

[33] O to realize space !
The plenteousness of all—that there are no bounds ;
To emerge, and be of the sky—of the sun and moon,
      and the flying clouds, as one with them.

[34] O the joy of a manly self-hood !
Personality—to be servile to none—to defer to none—
      not to any tyrant, known or unknown,
To walk with erect carriage, a step springy and elastic,
To look with calm gaze, or with a flashing eye,
To speak with a full and sonorous voice, out of a broad
      chest,
To confront with your personality all the other person-
      alities of the earth.

14

[35] Know'st thou the excellent joys of youth ?
Joys of the dear companions, and of the merry word,
      and laughing face ?
Joys of the glad, light-beaming day—joy of the wide-
      breath'd games ?
Joy of sweet music—joy of the lighted ball-room, and
      the dancers ?
Joy of the friendly, plenteous dinner—the strong
      carouse, and drinking ?

15

[36] Yet, O my soul supreme !
Know'st thou the joys of pensive thought ?
Joys of the free and lonesome heart—the tender,
      gloomy heart ?
Joy of the solitary walk—the spirit bowed yet proud—
      the suffering and the struggle ?

The agonistic throes, the extasies—joys of the solemn
    musings, day or night?
Joys of the thought of Death—the great spheres Time
    and Space?
Prophetic joys of better, loftier love's ideals—the Di-
    vine Wife—the sweet, eternal, perfect Comrade?
Joys all thine own, undying one—joys worthy thee, O
    Soul.

16

[37] O, while I live, to be the ruler of life—not a slave,
To meet life as a powerful conqueror,
No fumes—no ennui—no more complaints, or scornful
    criticisms.

[38] O me repellent and ugly!
To these proud laws of the air, the water, and the
    ground, proving my interior Soul impregnable,
And nothing exterior shall ever take command of me.

[39] O to attract by more than attraction!
How it is I know not—yet behold! the something
    which obeys none of the rest,
It is offensive, never defensive—yet how magnetic it
    draws.

17

[40] O joy of suffering!
To struggle against great odds! to meet enemies un-
    daunted!
To be entirely alone with them! to find how much one
    can stand!
To look strife, torture, prison, popular odium, death,
    face to face!
To mount the scaffold! to advance to the muzzles of
    guns with perfect nonchalance!
To be indeed a God!

18

[41] O, to sail to sea in a ship!
To leave this steady, unendurable land!
To leave the tiresome sameness of the streets, the side-
    walks and the houses;
To leave you, O you solid motionless land, and entering
    a ship,
To sail, and sail, and sail!

19

[42] O to have my life henceforth a poem of new joys!
To dance, clap hands, exult, shout, skip, leap, roll on,
    float on,
To be a sailor of the world, bound for all ports,
A ship itself, (see indeed these sails I spread to the sun
    and air,)
A swift and swelling ship, full of rich words—full of
    joys.

To Think of Time.

—

[1] To think of time—of all that retrospection!
To think of to-day, and the ages continued hencefor-
ward!

[2] Have you guess'd you yourself would not continue?
Have you dreaded these earth-beetles?
Have you fear'd the future would be nothing to you?

[3] Is to-day nothing? Is the beginningless past nothing?
If the future is nothing, they are just as surely nothing.

[4] To think that the sun rose in the east! that men and
women were flexible, real, alive! that everything
was alive!
To think that you and I did not see, feel, think, nor
bear our part!
To think that we are now here, and bear our part!

2

[5] Not a day passes—not a minute or second, without an
accouchement!
Not a day passes—not a minute or second, without a
corpse!

[6] The dull nights go over, and the dull days also,
The soreness of lying so much in bed goes over,
The physician, after long putting off, gives the silent
and terrible look for an answer.

The children come hurried and weeping, and the broth-
ers and sisters are sent for,
Medicines stand unused on the shelf—(the camphor-
smell has long pervaded the rooms,)
The faithful hand of the living does not desert the hand
of the dying,
The twitching lips press lightly on the forehead of the
dying,
The breath ceases, and the pulse of the heart ceases,
The corpse stretches on the bed, and the living look
upon it,
It is palpable as the living are palpable.

7 The living look upon the corpse with their eye-sight,
But without eye-sight lingers a different living, and
looks curiously on the corpse.

3

8 To think the thought of Death, merged in the thought
of materials!
To think that the rivers will flow, and the snow fall,
and fruits ripen, and act upon others as upon us
now—yet not act upon us!
To think of all these wonders of city and country, and
others taking great interest in them—and we
taking no interest in them!

9 To think how eager we are in building our houses!
To think others shall be just as eager, and we quite
indifferent!

10 (I see one building the house that serves him a few
years, or seventy or eighty years at most,
I see one building the house that serves him longer
than that.)

11 Slow-moving and black lines creep over the whole
earth—they never cease—they are the burial
lines,
He that was President was buried, and he that is now
President shall surely be buried.

4

[12] A reminiscence of the vulgar fate,
A frequent sample of the life and death of workmen,
Each after his kind :
Cold dash of waves at the ferry-wharf—posh and ice in
    the river, half-frozen mud in the streets, a gray
    discouraged sky overhead, the short last daylight
    of Twelfth-month,
A hearse and stages—other vehicles give place—the
    funeral of an old Broadway stage-driver, the
    cortege mostly drivers.

[13] Steady the trot to the cemetery, duly rattles the
    death-bell, the gate is pass'd, the new-dug grave
    is halted at, the living alight, the hearse uncloses,
The coffin is pass'd out, lower'd and settled, the whip is
    laid on the coffin, the earth is swiftly shovel'd in,
The mound above is flatted with the spades—silence,
A minute—no one moves or speaks—it is done,
He is decently put away—is there anything more ?

[14] He was a good fellow, free-mouth'd, quick-temper'd,
    not bad-looking, able to take his own part, witty,
    sensitive to a slight, ready with life or death for
    a friend, fond of women, gambled, ate hearty,
    drank hearty, had known what it was to be flush,
    grew low-spirited toward the last, sicken'd, was
    help'd by a contribution, died, aged forty-one
    years—and that was his funeral.

[15] Thumb extended, finger uplifted, apron, cape, gloves,
    strap, wet-weather clothes, whip carefully chosen,
    boss, spotter, starter, hostler, somebody loafing
    on you, you loafing on somebody, headway, man
    before and man behind, good day's work, bad
    day's work, pet stock, mean stock, first out, last
    out, turning-in at night ;
To think that these are so much and so nigh to other
    drivers—and he there takes no interest in them !

5

[16] The markets, the government, the working-man's
wages—to think what account they are through
our nights and days !
To think that other working-men will make just as
great account of them—yet we make little or no
account !

[17] The vulgar and the refined—what you call sin, and
what you call goodness—to think how wide a
difference !
To think the difference will still continue to others, yet
we lie beyond the difference.

[18] To think how much pleasure there is !
Have you pleasure from looking at the sky ? have you
pleasure from poems ?
Do you enjoy yourself in the city ? or engaged in business ? or planning a nomination and election ?
or with your wife and family ?
Or with your mother and sisters ? or in womanly housework ? or the beautiful maternal cares ?
—These also flow onward to others—you and I flow
onward,
But in due time, you and I shall take less interest in
them.

[19] Your farm, profits, crops,—to think how engross'd
you are !
To think there will still be farms, profits, crops—yet for
you, of what avail ?

6

[20] What will be, will be well—for what is, is well,
To take interest is well, and not to take interest shall
be well.

[21] The sky continues beautiful,
The pleasure of men with women shall never be sated,
nor the pleasure of women with men, nor the
pleasure from poems,

The domestic joys, the daily housework or business, the
    building of houses—these are not phantasms—
    they have weight, form, location ;
Farms, profits, crops, markets, wages, government, are
    none of them phantasms,
The difference between sin and goodness is no delusion,
The earth is not an echo—man and his life, and all the
    things of his life, are well-consider'd.

[22] You are not thrown to the winds—you gather cer-
    tainly and safely around yourself ;
Yourself ! Yourself ! Yourself, forever and ever !

7

[23] It is not to diffuse you that you were born of your
    mother and father—it is to identify you ;
It is not that you should be undecided, but that you
    should be decided ;
Something long preparing and formless is arrived and
    form'd in you,
You are henceforth secure, whatever comes or goes.

[24] The threads that were spun are gather'd, the weft
    crosses the warp, the pattern is systematic.

[25] The preparations have every one been justified,
The orchestra have sufficiently tuned their instruments
    —the baton has given the signal.

[26] The guest that was coming—he waited long, for rea-
    sons—he is now housed,
He is one of those who are beautiful and happy—he is
    one of those that to look upon and be with is
    enough.

[27] The law of the past cannot be eluded,
The law of the present and future cannot be eluded,
The law of the living cannot be eluded—it is eternal,
The law of promotion and transformation cannot be
    eluded.

The law of heroes and good-doers cannot be eluded,
The law of drunkards, informers, mean persons—not
    one iota thereof can be eluded.

8

[28] Slow moving and black lines go ceaselessly over the
    earth,
Northerner goes carried, and Southerner goes carried,
    and they on the Atlantic side, and they on the
    Pacific, and they between, and all through the
    Mississippi country, and all over the earth.

[29] The great masters and kosmos are well as they go—
    the heroes and good-doers are well,
The known leaders and inventors, and the rich owners
    and pious and distinguish'd, may be well,
But there is more account than that—there is strict
    account of all.

[30] The interminable hordes of the ignorant and wicked
    are not nothing,
The barbarians of Africa and Asia are not nothing,
The common people of Europe are not nothing—the
    American aborigines are not nothing,
The infected in the immigrant hospital are not nothing
    —the murderer or mean person is not nothing,
The perpetual successions of shallow people are not
    nothing as they go,
The lowest prostitute is not nothing—the mocker of
    religion is not nothing as he goes.

9

[31] Of and in all these things,
I have dream'd that we are not to be changed so much,
    nor the law of us changed,
I have dream'd that heroes and good-doers shall be
    under the present and past law,
And that murderers, drunkards, liars, shall be under
    the present and past law,
For I have dream'd that the law they are under now is
    enough.

[32] If otherwise, all came but to ashes of dung,
If maggots and rats ended us, then Alarum! for we are
    betray'd!
Then indeed suspicion of death.

[33] Do you suspect death? If I were to suspect death, I
    should die now,
Do you think I could walk pleasantly and well-suited
    toward annihilation?

10

[34] Pleasantly and well-suited I walk,
Whither I walk I cannot define, but I know it is good,
The whole universe indicates that it is good,
The past and the present indicate that it is good.

[25] How beautiful and perfect are the animals!
How perfect the earth, and the minutest thing upon it!
What is called good is perfect, and what is called bad is
    just as perfect,
The vegetables and minerals are all perfect, and the
    imponderable fluids are perfect;
Slowly and surely they have pass'd on to this, and
    slowly and surely they yet pass on.

11

[36] I swear I think now that everything without excep-
    tion has an eternal Soul!
The trees have, rooted in the ground! the weeds of the
    sea have! the animals!

[37] I swear I think there is nothing but immortality!
That the exquisite scheme is for it, and the nebulous
    float is for it, and the cohering is for it;
And all preparation is for it! and identity is for it! and
    life and materials are altogether for it!

CHANTING THE SQUARE DEIFIC.

1

CHANTING the square deific, out of the One advancing, out of the sides ;

Out of the old and new—out of the square entirely divine,

Solid, four-sided, (all the sides needed)...from this side JEHOVAH am I,

Old Brahm I, and I Saturnius am ;

Not Time affects me—I am Time, old, modern as any ;

Unpersuadable, relentless, executing righteous judgments ;

As the Earth, the Father, the brown old Kronos, with laws,

Aged beyond computation—yet ever new—ever with those mighty laws rolling,

Relentless, I forgive no man—whoever sins, dies—I will have that man's life ;

Therefore let none expect mercy—Have the seasons, gravitation, the appointed days, mercy?—No more have I ;

But as the seasons, and gravitation—and as all the appointed days, that forgive not,

I dispense from this side judgments inexorable, without the least remorse.

2

Consolator most mild, the promis'd one advancing,

With gentle hand extended—the mightier God am I,

Foretold by prophets and poets, in their most rapt prophecies and poems ;

From this side, lo ! the Lord CHRIST gazes—lo ! Hermes I—lo ! mine is Hercules' face ;

All sorrow, labor, suffering, I, tallying it, absorb in myself ;

Many times have I been rejected, taunted, put in prison, and crucified—and many times shall be again ;

All the world have I given up for my dear brothers'
    and sisters' sake—for the soul's sake ;
Wending my way through the homes of men, rich or
    poor, with the kiss of affection ;
For I am affection—I am the cheer-bringing God, with
    hope, and all-enclosing Charity ;
(Conqueror yet—for before me all the armies and sol-
    diers of the earth shall yet bow—and all the
    weapons of war become impotent :)
With indulgent words, as to children—with fresh and
    sane words, mine only ;
Young and strong I pass, knowing well I am destin'd
    myself to an early death :
But my Charity has no death—my Wisdom dies not,
    neither early nor late,
And my sweet Love, bequeath'd here and elsewhere,
    never dies.

3

Aloof, dissatisfied, plotting revolt,
Comrade of criminals, brother of slaves,
Crafty, despised, a drudge, ignorant,
With sudra face and worn brow, black, but in the depths
    of my heart, proud as any ;
Lifted, now and always, against whoever, scorning,
    assumes to rule me ;
Morose, full of guile, full of reminiscences, brooding,
    with many wiles,
(Though it was thought I was baffled and dispell'd,
    and my wiles done—but that will never be ;)
Defiant, I, SATAN, still live—still utter words—in new
    lands duly appearing, (and old ones also ;)
Permanent here, from my side, warlike, equal with any,
    real as any,
Nor time, nor change, shall ever change me or my words.

4

Santa SPIRITA, breather, life,
Beyond the light, lighter than light,

Beyond the flames of hell—joyous, leaping easily above
    hell ;
Beyond Paradise—perfumed solely with mine own
    perfume ;
Including all life on earth—touching, including God—
    including Saviour and Satan ;
Ethereal, pervading all, (for without me, what were all ?
    what were God?)
Essence of forms—life of the real identities, permanent,
    positive, (namely the unseen,)
Life of the great round world, the sun and stars, and of
    man—I, the general Soul,
Here the square finishing, the solid, I the most solid,
Breathe my breath also through these songs.

WHISPERS

OF

HEAVENLY DEATH.

—

WHISPERS OF HEAVENLY DEATH.

[1] WHISPERS of heavenly death, murmur'd I hear ;
Labial gossip of night—sibilant chorals ;
Footsteps gently ascending—mystical breezes, wafted
    soft and low ;
Ripples of unseen rivers—tides of a current, flowing,
    forever flowing ;
(Or is it the plashing of tears? the measureless waters
    of human tears?)

[2] I see, just see, skyward, great cloud-masses ;
Mournfully, slowly they roll, silently swelling and mix-
    ing ;
With, at times, a half-dimm'd, sadden'd, far-off star,
Appearing and disappearing.

[3] (Some parturition, rather—some solemn, immortal
    birth :
On the frontiers, to eyes impenetrable,
Some Soul is passing over.)

DAREST THOU NOW, O SOUL.

1

DAREST thou now, O Soul,
Walk out with me toward the Unknown Region,
Where neither ground is for the feet, nor any path to
      follow ?

2

No map, there, nor guide,
Nor voice sounding, nor touch of human hand,
Nor face with blooming flesh, nor lips, nor eyes, are in
      that land.

3

I know it not, O Soul ;
Nor dost thou—all is a blank before us ;
All waits, undream'd of, in that region—that inaccessi-
      ble land.

4

Till, when the ties loosen,
All but the ties eternal, Time and Space,
Nor darkness, gravitation, sense, nor any bounds, bound
      us.

5

Then we burst forth—we float,
In Time and Space, O Soul—prepared for them ;
Equal, equipt at last—(O joy ! O fruit of all !) them to
      fulfil, O Soul.

———

OF HIM I LOVE DAY AND NIGHT.

OF him I love day and night, I dream'd I heard he was
      dead ;
And I dream'd I went where they had buried him I
      love—but he was not in that place ;
And I dream'd I wander'd, searching among burial-
      places, to find him ;

And I found that every place was a burial place ;
The houses full of life were equally full of death, (this
    house is now ;)
The streets, the shipping, the places of amusement, the
    Chicago, Boston, Philadelphia, the Mannahatta,
    were as full of the dead as of the living,
And fuller, O vastly fuller, of the dead than of the
    living ;
—And what I dream'd I will henceforth tell to every
    person and age,
And I stand henceforth bound to what I dream'd ;
And now I am willing to disregard burial-places, and
    dispense with them ;
And if the memorials of the dead were put up indiffer-
    ently everywhere, even in the room where I eat
    or sleep, I should be satisfied ;
And if the corpse of any one I love, or if my own corpse,
    be duly render'd to powder, and pour'd in the
    sea, I shall be satisfied ;
Or if it be distributed to the winds, I shall be satisfied.

ASSURANCES.

I NEED no assurances—I am a man who is preoccupied,
    of his own Soul ;
I do not doubt that from under the feet, and beside the
    hands and face I am cognizant of, are now look-
    ing faces I am not cognizant of—calm and actual
    faces ;
I do not doubt but the majesty and beauty of the world
    are latent in any iota of the world ;
I do not doubt I am limitless, and that the universes
    are limitless—in vain I try to think how limitless ;
I do not doubt that the orbs, and the systems of orbs,
    play their swift sports through the air on pur-
    pose—and that I shall one day be eligible to do
    as much as they, and more than they ;

I do not doubt that temporary affairs keep on and on,
    millions of years ;
I do not doubt interiors have their interiors, and exte-
    riors have their exteriors—and that the eye-sight
    has another eye-sight, and the hearing another
    hearing, and the voice another voice ;
I do not doubt that the passionately-wept deaths of
    young men are provided for—and that the deaths
    of young women, and the deaths of little children,
    are provided for ;
(Did you think Life was so well provided for—and
    Death, the purport of all Life, is not well pro-
    vided for ?)
I do not doubt that wrecks at sea, no matter what the
    horrors of them—no matter whose wife, child,
    husband, father, lover, has gone down, are pro-
    vided for, to the minutest points ;
I do not doubt that whatever can possibly happen, any
    where, at any time, is provided for, in the inher-
    ences of things ;
I do not think Life provides for all, and for Time and
    Space—but I believe Heavenly Death provides
    for all.

YET, YET, YE DOWNCAST HOURS.

1

Yet, yet, ye downcast hours, I know ye also ;
Weights of lead, how ye clog and cling at my ankles!
Earth to a chamber of mourning turns—I hear the
    o'erweening, mocking voice,
Matter is conqueror—matter, triumphant only, continues
    onward.

2

Despairing cries float ceaselessly toward me,
The call of my nearest lover, putting forth, alarm'd,
    uncertain.

The Sea I am quickly to sail, come tell me,
Come tell me where I am speeding—tell me my destination.

3

I understand your anguish, but I cannot help you,
I approach, hear, behold—the sad mouth, the look out
    of the eyes, your mute inquiry,
Whither I go from the bed I recline on, come tell me:
Old age, alarm'd, uncertain—A young woman's voice,
    appealing to me for comfort ;
A young man's voice, *Shall I not escape ?*

QUICKSAND YEARS.

QUICKSAND years that whirl me I know not whither,
Your schemes, politics, fail—lines give way—substances
    mock and elude me ;
Only the theme I sing, the great and strong-possess'd
    Soul, eludes not ;
One's-self must never give way—that is the final sub-
    stance—that out of all is sure ;
Out of politics, triumphs, battles, life—what at last
    finally remains ?
When shows break up, what but One's-Self is sure ?

THAT MUSIC ALWAYS ROUND ME.

THAT music always round me, unceasing, unbeginning
    —yet long untaught I did not hear ;
But now the chorus I hear, and am elated ;
A tenor, strong, ascending, with power and health, with
    glad notes of day-break I hear,
A soprano, at intervals, sailing buoyantly over the tops
    of immense waves.

A transparent base, shuddering lusciously under and
     through the universe,
The triumphant tutti—the funeral wailings, with sweet
     flutes and violins—all these I fill myself with ;
I hear not the volumes of sound merely—I am moved
     by the exquisite meanings,
I listen to the different voices winding in and out,
     striving, contending with fiery vehemence to
     excel each other in emotion ;
I do not think the performers know themselves—but
     now I think I begin to know them.

AS IF A PHANTOM CARESS'D ME.

As if a phantom caress'd me,
I thought I was not alone, walking here by the shore ;
But the one I thought was with me, as now I walk by
     the shore—the one I loved, that caress'd me,
As I lean and look through the glimmering light—that
     one has utterly disappear'd,
And those appear that are hateful to me, and mock me.

HERE, SAILOR !

WHAT ship, puzzled at sea, cons for the true reckon-
     ing?
Or, coming in, to avoid the bars, and follow the chan-
     nel, a perfect pilot needs?
Here, sailor ! Here, ship ! take aboard the most perfect
     pilot,
Whom, in a little boat, putting off, and rowing, I,
     hailing you, offer.

A NOISELESS, PATIENT SPIDER.

1 A NOISELESS patient spider,
I mark'd, where, on a little promontory, it stood, isolated ;
Mark'd how, to explore the vacant, vast surrounding,
It launch'd forth filament, filament, filament, out of itself ;
Ever unreeling them—ever tirelessly speeding them.

2 And you, O my Soul, where you stand,
Surrounded, surrounded, in measureless oceans of space,
Ceaselessly musing, venturing, throwing,—seeking the spheres, to connect them ;
Till the bridge you will need, be form'd—till the ductile anchor hold ;
Till the gossamer thread you fling, catch somewhere, O my Soul.

THE LAST INVOCATION.

1

AT the last, tenderly,
From the walls of the powerful, fortress'd house,
From the clasp of the knitted locks—from the keep of the well-closed doors,
Let me be wafted.

2

Let me glide noiselessly forth ;
With the key of softness unlock the locks—with a whisper,
Set ope the doors, O Soul !

3

Tenderly ! be not impatient !
(Strong is your hold, O mortal flesh !
Strong is your hold, O love.)

AS I WATCH'D THE PLOUGHMAN PLOUGH-ING.

As I watch'd the ploughman ploughing,
Or the sower sowing in the fields—or the harvester
    harvesting,
I saw there too, O life and death, your analogies :
(Life, life is the tillage, and Death is the harvest accord-
    ing.)

PENSIVE AND FALTERING.

Pensive and faltering,
The words, *the dead*, I write ;
For living are the Dead ;
(Haply the only living, only real,
And I the apparition—I the spectre.)

SEA-SHORE MEMORIES.

OUT OF THE CRADLE ENDLESSLY ROCKING.

1

[1] Out of the cradle endlessly rocking,
Out of the mocking-bird's throat, the musical shuttle,
Out of the Ninth-month midnight,
Over the sterile sands, and the fields beyond, where the
　　　child, leaving his bed, wander'd alone, bare-
　　　headed, barefoot,
Down from the shower'd halo,
Up from the mystic play of shadows, twining and twist-
　　　ing as if they were alive,
Out from the patches of briers and blackberries,
From the memories of the bird that chanted to me,
From your memories, sad brother—from the fitful
　　　risings and fallings I heard,
From under that yellow half-moon, late-risen, and
　　　swollen as if with tears,
From those beginning notes of sickness and love, there
　　　in the transparent mist,
From the thousand responses of my heart, never to
　　　cease,
From the myriad thence-arous'd words,
From the word stronger and more delicious than any,
From such, as now they start, the scene revisiting,
As a flock, twittering, rising, or overhead passing,
Borne hither—ere all eludes me, hurriedly,
A man—yet by these tears a little boy again,

Throwing myself on the sand, confronting the waves,
I, chanter of pains and joys, uniter of here and hereafter,
Taking all hints to use them—but swiftly leaping
      beyond them,
A reminiscence sing.

2

[2] Once, Paumanok,
When the snows had melted—when the lilac-scent was
      in the air, and the Fifth-month grass was
      growing,
Up this sea-shore, in some briers,
Two guests from Alabama—two together,
And their nest, and four light-green eggs, spotted with
      brown,
And every day the he-bird, to and fro, near at hand,
And every day the she-bird, crouch'd on her nest, silent,
      with bright eyes,
And every day I, a curious boy, never too close, never
      disturbing them,
Cautiously peering, absorbing, translating.

3

[3] *Shine! shine! shine!*
Pour down your warmth, great Sun!
While we bask—we two together.

[4] *Two together!*
Winds blow South, or winds blow North,
Day come white, or night come black,
Home, or rivers and mountains from home,
Singing all time, minding no time,
While we two keep together.

4

[5] Till of a sudden,
May-be kill'd, unknown to her mate,
One forenoon the she-bird crouch'd not on the nest,
Nor return'd that afternoon, nor the next,
Nor ever appear'd again.

⁶ And thenceforward, all summer, in the sound of the
sea,
And at night, under the full of the moon, in calmer
weather,
Over the hoarse surging of the sea,
Or flitting from brier to brier by day,
I saw, I heard at intervals, the remaining one, the he-
bird,
The solitary guest from Alabama.

5

⁷ *Blow! blow! blow!*
Blow up, sea-winds, along Paumanok's shore!
I wait and I wait, till you blow my mate to me.

6

⁸ Yes, when the stars glisten'd,
All night long, on the prong of a moss-scallop'd stake,
Down, almost amid the slapping waves,
Sat the lone singer, wonderful, causing tears.

⁹ He call'd on his mate ;
He pour'd forth the meanings which I, of all men, know.

¹⁰ Yes, my brother, I know ;
The rest might not—but I have treasur'd every note ;
For once, and more than once, dimly, down to the
beach gliding,
Silent, avoiding the moonbeams, blending myself with
the shadows,
Recalling now the obscure shapes, the echoes, the
sounds and sights after their sorts,
The white arms out in the breakers tirelessly tossing,
I, with bare feet, a child, the wind wafting my hair,
Listen'd long and long.

¹¹ Listen'd, to keep, to sing—now translating the notes,
Following you, my brother.
4

7

[12] *Soothe! soothe! soothe!*
Close on its wave soothes the wave behind,
And again another behind, embracing and lapping, every
      one close,
But my love soothes not me, not me.

[13] *Low hangs the moon—it rose late;*
O it is lagging—O I think it is heavy with love, with love.

[14] *O madly the sea pushes, pushes upon the land,*
With love—with love.

[15] *O night! do I not see my love fluttering out there among*
      the breakers?
What is that little black thing I see there in the white?

[16] *Loud! loud! loud!*
Loud I call to you, my love!
High and clear I shoot my voice over the waves;
Surely you must know who is here, is here;
You must know who I am, my love.

[17] *Low-hanging moon!*
What is that dusky spot in your brown yellow?
O it is the shape, the shape of my mate!
O moon, do not keep her from me any longer.

[18] *Land! land! O land!*
Whichever way I turn, O I think you could give me my
      mate back again, if you only would;
For I am almost sure I see her dimly whichever way I look.

[19] *O rising stars!*
Perhaps the one I want so much will rise, will rise with
      some of you.

[20] *O throat! O trembling throat!*
Sound clearer through the atmosphere!
Pierce the woods, the earth;
Somewhere listening to catch you, must be the one I want.

²¹ *Shake out, carols !*
Solitary here—the night's carols !
Carols of lonesome love ! Death's carols !
Carols under that lagging, yellow, waning moon !
O, under that moon, where she droops almost down into the
        sea !
O reckless, despairing carols.

²² *But soft ! sink low ;*
Soft ! let me just murmur ;
And do you wait a moment, you husky-noised sea ;
For somewhere I believe I heard my mate responding to
        me,
So faint—I must be still, be still to listen ;
But not altogether still, for then she might not come imme-
        diately to me.

²³ *Hither, my love !*
Here I am ! Here !
With this just-sustain'd note I announce myself to you ;
This gentle call is for you, my love, for you.

²⁴ *Do not be decoy'd elsewhere !*
That is the whistle of the wind—it is not my voice ;
That is the fluttering, the fluttering of the spray ;
Those are the shadows of leaves.

²⁵ *O darkness ! O in vain !*
O I am very sick and sorrowful.

²⁶ *O brown halo in the sky, near the moon, drooping upon*
        the sea !
O troubled reflection in the sea !
O throat ! O throbbing heart !
O all—and I singing uselessly, uselessly all the night.

²⁷ *Yet I murmur, murmur on !*
O murmurs—you yourselves make me continue to sing, I
        know not why.

[28] *O past ! O life ! O songs of joy !*
In the air—in the woods—over fields ;
Loved ! loved ! loved ! loved ! loved !
But my love no more, no more with me !
We two together no more.

8

[29] The aria sinking ;
All else continuing—the stars shining,
The winds blowing—the notes of the bird continuous
    echoing,
With angry moans the fierce old mother incessantly
    moaning,
On the sands of Paumanok's shore, gray and rustling ;
The yellow half-moon enlarged, sagging down, droop-
    ing, the face of the sea almost touching ;
The boy extatic—with his bare feet the waves, with his
    hair the atmosphere dallying,
The love in the heart long pent, now loose, now at last
    tumultuously bursting,
The aria's meaning, the ears, the Soul, swiftly deposit-
    ing,
The strange tears down the cheeks coursing,
The colloquy there—the trio—each uttering,
The undertone — the savage old mother, incessantly
    crying,
To the boy's Soul's questions sullenly timing—some
    drown'd secret hissing,
To the outsetting bard of love.

9

[30] Demon or bird ! (said the boy's soul,)
Is it indeed toward your mate you sing ? or is it mostly
    to me ?
For I, that was a child, my tongue's use sleeping,
Now I have heard you,
Now in a moment I know what I am for—I awake,
And already a thousand singers—a thousand songs,
    clearer, louder and more sorrowful than yours,

A thousand warbling echoes have started to life within
    me,
Never to die.

³¹ O you singer, solitary, singing by yourself—project-
    ing me ;
O solitary me, listening—never more shall I cease per-
    petuating you ;
Never more shall I escape, never more the reverbera-
    tions,
Never more the cries of unsatisfied love be absent from
    me,
Never again leave me to be the peaceful child I was
    before what there, in the night,
By the sea, under the yellow and sagging moon,
The messenger there arous'd—the fire, the sweet hell
    within,
The unknown want, the destiny of me.

³² O give me the clew ! (it lurks in the night here some-
    where ;)
O if I am to have so much, let me have more !
O a word ! O what is my destination ? (I fear it is hence-
    forth chaos ;)
O how joys, dreads, convolutions, human shapes, and all
    shapes, spring as from graves around me !
O phantoms ! you cover all the land and all the sea !
O I cannot see in the dimness whether you smile or
    frown upon me ;
O vapor, a look, a word ! O well-beloved !
O you dear women's and men's phantoms !

³³ A word then, (for I will conquer it,)
The word final, superior to all,
Subtle, sent up—what is it ?—I listen ;
Are you whispering it, and have been all the time, you
    sea-waves ?
Is that it from your liquid rims and wet sands ?

10

[34] Whereto answering, the sea,
Delaying not, hurrying not,
Whisper'd me through the night, and very plainly be-
    fore daybreak,
Lisp'd to me the low and delicious word Death ;
And again Death—ever Death, Death, Death,
Hissing melodious, neither like the bird, nor like my
    arous'd child's heart,
But edging near, as privately for me, rustling at my
    feet,
Creeping thence steadily up to my ears, and laving me
    softly all over,
Death, Death, Death, Death, Death.

[35] Which I do not forget,
But fuse the song of my dusky demon and brother,
That he sang to me in the moonlight on Paumanok's
    gray beach,
With the thousand responsive songs, at random,
My own songs, awaked from that hour ;
And with them the key, the word up from the waves,
The word of the sweetest song, and all songs,
That strong and delicious word which, creeping to my
    feet,
The sea whisper'd me.

ELEMENTAL DRIFTS.

1

[1] Elemental drifts !
How I wish I could impress others as you have just
    been impressing me !

[2] As I ebb'd with an ebb of the ocean of life,
As I wended the shores I know.

As I walk'd where the ripples continually wash you,
Paumanok,
Where they rustle up, hoarse and sibilant,
Where the fierce old mother endlessly cries for her
castaways,
I, musing, late in the autumn day, gazing off south-
ward,
Alone, held by this eternal Self of me, out of the pride
of which I utter my poems,
Was seiz'd by the spirit that trails in the lines under-
foot,
In the rim, the sediment, that stands for all the water
and all the land of the globe.

[3] Fascinated, my eyes, reverting from the south, dropt,
to follow those slender winrows,
Chaff, straw, splinters of wood, weeds, and the sea-
gluten,
Scum, scales from shining rocks, leaves of salt-lettuce,
left by the tide :
Miles walking, the sound of breaking waves the other
side of me,
Paumanok, there and then, as I thought the old
thought of likenesses,
These you presented to me, you fish-shaped island,
As I wended the shores I know,
As I walk'd with that eternal Self of me, seeking types.

2

[4] As I wend to the shores I know not,
As I list to the dirge, the voices of men and women
wreck'd,
As I inhale the impalpable breezes that set in upon
me,
As the ocean so mysterious rolls toward me closer and
closer,
I, too, but signify, at the utmost, a little wash'd-up
drift,
A few sands and dead leaves to gather,
Gather, and merge myself as part of the sands and
drift.

⁵ O baffled, balk'd, bent to the very earth,
Oppress'd with myself that I have dared to open my
    mouth,
Aware now, that, amid all that blab whose echoes recoil
    upon me, I have not once had the least idea
    who or what I am,
But that before all my insolent poems the real ME
    stands yet untouch'd, untold, altogether un-
    reach'd,
Withdrawn far, mocking me with mock-congratulatory
    signs and bows,
With peals of distant ironical laughter at every word I
    have written,
Pointing in silence to these songs, and then to the sand
    beneath.

⁶ Now I perceive I have not understood anything—not
    a single object—and that no man ever can.

⁷ I perceive Nature, here in sight of the sea, is taking
    advantage of me, to dart upon me, and sting me,
Because I have dared to open my mouth to sing at all.

3

⁸ You oceans both! I close with you ;
We murmur alike reproachfully, rolling our sands and
    drift, knowing not why,
These little shreds indeed, standing for you and me
    and all.

⁹ You friable shore, with trails of debris !
You fish-shaped island ! I take what is underfoot ;
What is yours is mine, my father.

¹⁰ I too Paumanok,
I too have bubbled up, floated the measureless float,
    and been wash'd on your shores ;
I too am but a trail of drift and debris,
I too leave little wrecks upon you, you fish-shaped
    island.

¹¹ I throw myself upon your breast, my father,
I cling to you so that you cannot unloose me,
I hold you so firm, till you answer me something.

¹² Kiss me, my father,
Touch me with your lips, as I touch those I love,
Breathe to me, while I hold you close, the secret of the
    murmuring I envy.

4

¹³ Ebb, ocean of life, (the flow will return,)
Cease not your moaning, you fierce old mother,
Endlessly cry for your castaways—but fear not, deny
    not me,
Rustle not up so hoarse and angry against my feet, as I
    touch you, or gather from you.

¹⁴ I mean tenderly by you and all,
I gather for myself, and for this phantom, looking down
    where we lead, and following me and mine.

¹⁵ Me and mine!
We, loose winrows, little corpses,
Froth, snowy white, and bubbles,
(See! from my dead lips the ooze exuding at last!
See—the prismatic colors, glistening and rolling!)
Tufts of straw, sands, fragments,
Buoy'd hither from many moods, one contradicting
    another,
From the storm, the long calm, the darkness, the swell;
Musing, pondering, a breath, a briny tear, a dab of
    liquid or soil;
Up just as much out of fathomless workings fermented
    and thrown;
A limp blossom or two, torn, just as much over waves
    floating, drifted at random;
Just as much for us that sobbing dirge of Nature;
Just as much, whence we come, that blare of the cloud-
    trumpets;

We, capricious, brought hither, we know not whence,
    spread out before you,
You, up there, walking or sitting,
Whoever you are—we too lie in drifts at your feet.

TEARS.

TEARS! tears! tears!
In the night, in solitude, tears;
On the white shore dripping, dripping, suck'd in by the
    sand;
Tears—not a star shining—all dark and desolate;
Moist tears from the eyes of a muffled head:
—O who is that ghost?—that form in the dark, with
    tears?
What shapeless lump is that, bent, crouch'd there on
    the sand?
Streaming tears—sobbing tears—throes, choked with
    wild cries;
O storm, embodied, rising, careering, with swift steps
    along the beach;
O wild and dismal night storm, with wind! O belching
    and desperate!
O shade, so sedate and decorous by day, with calm
    countenance and regulated pace;
But away, at night, as you fly, none looking—O then
    the unloosen'd ocean,
Of tears! tears! tears!

ABOARD, AT A SHIP'S HELM.

[1] ABOARD, at a ship's helm,
A young steersman, steering with care.

[2] A bell through fog on a sea-coast dolefully ringing,
An ocean-bell—O a warning bell, rock'd by the waves.

³ O you give good notice indeed, you bell by the sea-
      reefs ringing,
Ringing, ringing, to warn the ship from its wreck-place.

⁴ For, as on the alert, O steersman, you mind the bell's
      admonition,
The bows turn,—the freighted ship, tacking, speeds
      away under her gray sails,
The beautiful and noble ship, with all her precious
      wealth, speeds away gaily and safe.

⁵ But O the ship, the immortal ship! O ship aboard the
      ship!
O ship of the body—ship of the soul—voyaging, voyag-
      ing, voyaging.

ON THE BEACH, AT NIGHT.

1

¹ On the beach, at night,
Stands a child, with her father,
Watching the east, the autumn sky.

² Up through the darkness,
While ravening clouds, the burial clouds, in black
      masses spreading,
Lower, sullen and fast, athwart and down the sky,
Amid a transparent clear belt of ether yet left in the
      east,
Ascends, large and calm, the lord-star Jupiter;
And nigh at hand, only a very little above,
Swim the delicate brothers, the Pleiades.

2

³ From the beach, the child, holding the hand of her
      father,
Those burial-clouds that lower, victorious, soon to de-
      vour all,
Watching, silently weeps.

4 Weep not, child,
Weep not, my darling,
With these kisses let me remove your tears ;
The ravening clouds shall not long be victorious,
They shall not long possess the sky—shall devour the
　　stars only in apparition :
Jupiter shall emerge—be patient—watch again another
　　night—the Pleiades shall emerge,
They are immortal—all those stars, both silvery and
　　golden, shall shine out again,
The great stars and the little ones shall shine out again
　　—they endure ;
The vast immortal suns, and the long-enduring pensive
　　moons, shall again shine.

3

5 Then, dearest child, mournest thou only for Jupiter?
Considerest thou alone the burial of the stars ?

6 Something there is,
(With my lips soothing thee, adding, I whisper,
I give thee the first suggestion, the problem and indi-
　　rection,)
Something there is more immortal even than the stars,
(Many the burials, many the days and nights, passing
　　away,)
Something that shall endure longer even than lustrous
　　Jupiter,
Longer than sun, or any revolving satellite,
Or the radiant brothers, the Pleiades.

THE WORLD BELOW THE BRINE.

The world below the brine ;
Forests at the bottom of the sea—the branches and
　　leaves,
Sea-lettuce, vast lichens, strange flowers and seeds—
　　the thick tangle, the openings, and the pink turf,

Different colors, pale gray and green, purple, white,
and gold—the play of light through the water,
Dumb swimmers there among the rocks—coral, gluten,
grass, rushes—and the aliment of the swimmers,
Sluggish existences grazing there, suspended, or slowly
crawling close to the bottom,
The sperm-whale at the surface, blowing air and spray,
or disporting with his flukes,
The leaden-eyed shark, the walrus, the turtle, the hairy
sea-leopard, and the sting-ray ;
Passions there—wars, pursuits, tribes—sight in those
ocean-depths — breathing that thick-breathing
air, as so many do ;
The change thence to the sight here, and to the subtle
air breathed by beings like us, who walk this
sphere ;
The change onward from ours, to that of beings who
walk other spheres.

ON THE BEACH AT NIGHT ALONE.

¹ ON the beach at night alone,
As the old mother sways her to and fro, singing her
husky song,
As I watch the bright stars shining—I think a thought
of the clef of the universes, and of the future.

² A VAST SIMILITUDE interlocks all,
All spheres, grown, ungrown, small, large, suns, moons,
planets, comets, asteroids,
All the substances of the same, and all that is spiritual
upon the same,
All distances of place, however wide,
All distances of time—all inanimate forms,
All Souls—all living bodies, though they be ever so
different, or in different worlds,
All gaseous, watery, vegetable, mineral processes—the
fishes. the brutes.

All men and women—me also ;
All nations, colors, barbarisms, civilizations, languages ;
All identities that have existed, or may exist, on this
    globe, or any globe ;
All lives and deaths—all of the past, present, future ;
This vast similitude spans them, and always has spann'd,
    and shall forever span them, and compactly hold
    them, and enclose them.

Leaves of Grass.

A CAROL OF HARVEST, FOR 1867.

[In all History, antique or modern, the grandest achievement
yet for political Humanity—grander even than the triumph of
THIS UNION over Secession—was the return, disbanding, and
peaceful disintegration from compact military organization, back
into agricultural and civil employments, of the vast Armies, the
two millions of embattled men of America—a problem reserved
for Democracy, our day and land, to promptly solve.]

1

¹ A SONG of the good green grass!
A song no more of the city streets;
A song of farms—a song of the soil of fields.

² A song with the smell of sun-dried hay, where the
       nimble pitchers handle the pitch-fork;
A song tasting of new wheat, and of fresh-husk'd maize.

2

³ For the lands, and for these passionate days, and for
       myself,
Now I awhile return to thee, O soil of Autumn fields,
Reclining on thy breast, giving myself to thee,
Answering the pulses of thy sane and equable heart,
Tuning a verse for thee.

⁴ O Earth, that hast no voice, confide to me a voice!
O harvest of my lands! O boundless summer growths!
O lavish, brown, parturient earth! O infinite, teeming
       womb!
A verse to seek, to see, to narrate thee.

3

[5] Ever upon this stage,
Is acted God's calm, annual drama,
Gorgeous processions, songs of birds,
Sunrise, that fullest feeds and freshens most the soul,
The heaving sea, the waves upon the shore, the musical,
    strong waves,
The woods, the stalwart trees, the slender, tapering
    trees,
The flowers, the grass, the lilliput, countless armies of
    the grass,
The heat, the showers, the measureless pasturages,
The scenery of the snows, the winds' free orchestra,
The stretching, light-hung roof of clouds—the clear
    cerulean, and the bulging, silvery fringes,
The high dilating stars, the placid, beckoning stars,
The moving flocks and herds, the plains and emerald
    meadows,
The shows of all the varied lands, and all the growths
    and products.

4

[6] Fecund America! To day,
Thou art all over set in births and joys!
Thou groan'st with riches! thy wealth clothes thee as
    with a swathing garment!
Thou laughest loud with ache of great possessions!
A myriad-twining life, like interlacing vines, binds all
    thy vast demesne!
As some huge ship, freighted to water's edge, thou
    ridest into port!
As rain falls from the heaven, and vapors rise from
    earth, so have the precious values fallen upon
    thee, and risen out of thee!
Thou envy of the globe! thou miracle!
Thou, bathed, choked, swimming in plenty!
Thou lucky Mistress of the tranquil barns!
Thou Prairie Dame that sittest in the middle, and
    lookest out upon thy world, and lookest East,
    and lookest West!

Dispensatress, that by a word givest a thousand miles
—that giv'st a million farms, and missest nothing!
Thou All-Acceptress—thou Hospitable—(thou only art
hospitable, as God is hospitable.)

5

[7] When late I sang, sad was my voice;
Sad were the shows around me, with deafening noises
of hatred, and smoke of conflict;
In the midst of the armies, the Heroes, I stood,
Or pass'd with slow step through the wounded and
dying.

[8] But now I sing not War,
Nor the measur'd march of soldiers, nor the tents of
camps,
Nor the regiments hastily coming up, deploying in line
of battle.

[9] No more the dead and wounded;
No more the sad, unnatural shows of War.

[10] Ask'd room those flush'd immortal ranks? the first
forth-stepping armies?
Ask room, alas, the ghastly ranks—the armies dread
that follow'd.

6

[11] (Pass—pass, ye proud brigades!
So handsome, dress'd in blue—with your tramping,
sinewy legs;
With your shoulders young and strong—with your
knapsacks and your muskets;
—How elate I stood and watch'd you, where, starting
off, you march'd!

[12] Pass;—then rattle, drums, again!
Scream, you steamers on the river, out of whistles loud
and shrill, your salutes!

For an army heaves in sight—O another gathering
    army!
Swarming, trailing on the rear—O you dread, accruing
    army!
O you regiments so piteous, with your mortal diarrhœa!
    with your fever!
O my land's maimed darlings! with the plenteous bloody
    bandage and the crutch!
Lo! your pallid army follow'd!)

7

[13] But on these days of brightness,
On the far-stretching beauteous landscape, the roads
    and lanes, the high-piled farm-wagons, and the
    fruits and barns,
Shall the dead intrude?

[14] Ah, the dead to me mar not—they fit well in Na-
    ture;
They fit very well in the landscape, under the trees and
    grass,
And along the edge of the sky, in the horizon's far
    margin.

[15] Nor do I forget you, departed;
Nor in winter or summer, my lost ones;
But most, in the open air, as now, when my soul is
    rapt and at peace—like pleasing phantoms,
Your dear memories, rising, glide silently by me.

8

[16] I saw the day, the return of the Heroes;
(Yet the Heroes never surpass'd, shall never return;
Them, that day, I saw not.)

[17] I saw the interminable Corps—I saw the processions
    of armies,
I saw them approaching, defiling by, with divisions,
Streaming northward, their work done, camping awhile
    in clusters of mighty camps.

[18] No holiday soldiers!—youthful, yet veterans ;
Worn, swart, handsome, strong, of the stock of home-
    stead and workshop,
Harden'd of many a long campaign and sweaty march,
Inured on many a hard-fought, bloody field.

9

[19] A pause—the armies wait ;
A million flush'd, embattled conquerors wait ;
The world, too, waits—then, soft as breaking night, and
    sure as dawn,
They melt—they disappear.

[20] Exult, indeed, O lands! victorious lands !
Not there your victory, on those red, shuddering fields ;
But here and hence your victory.

[21] Melt, melt away, ye armies! disperse, ye blue-clad
    soldiers !
Resolve ye back again—give up, for good, your deadly
    arms ;
Other the arms, the fields henceforth for you, or South
    or North, or East or West,
With saner wars—sweet wars—life-giving wars.

10

[22] Loud, O my throat, and clear, O soul !
The season of thanks, and the voice of full-yielding ;
The chant of joy and power for boundless fertility.

[23] All till'd and untill'd fields expand before me ;
I see the true arenas of my race—or first, or last,
Man's innocent and strong arenas.

[24] I see the Heroes at other toils ;
I see, well-wielded in their hands, the better weapons.

11

[25] I see where America, Mother of All,
Well-pleased, with full-spanning eye, gazes forth, dwells
         long,
And counts the varied gathering of the products.

[26] Busy the far, the sunlit panorama ;
Prairie, orchard, and yellow grain of the North,
Cotton and rice of the South, and Louisianian cane ;
Open, unseeded fallows, rich fields of clover and tim-
         othy,
Kine and horses feeding, and droves of sheep and
         swine,
And many a stately river flowing, and many a jocund
         brook,
And healthy uplands with their herby-perfumed breezes,
And the good green grass—that delicate miracle, the
         ever-recurring grass.

12

[27] Toil on, Heroes ! harvest the products !
Not alone on those warlike fields, the Mother of All,
With dilated form and lambent eyes, watch'd you.

[28] Toil on, Heroes ! toil well ! Handle the weapons
         well !
The Mother of All—yet here, as ever, she watches
         you.

[29] Well-pleased, America, thou beholdest,
Over the fields of the West, those crawling monsters,
The human-divine inventions, the labor-saving imple-
         ments :
Beholdest, moving in every direction, imbued as with
         life, the revolving hay-rakes,
The steam-power reaping-machines, and the horse-power
         machines.

The engines, thrashers of grain, and cleaners of grain,
   well separating the straw—the nimble work of
   the patent pitch-fork ;
Beholdest the newer saw-mill, the southern cotton-gin,
   and the rice-cleanser.

[30] Beneath thy look, O Maternal,
With these, and else, and with their own strong hands,
   the Heroes harvest.

[31] All gather, and all harvest ;
(Yet but for thee, O Powerful ! not a scythe might
   swing, as now, in security ;
Not a maize-stalk dangle, as now, its silken tassels in
   peace.)

13

[32] Under Thee only they harvest—even but a wisp of
   hay, under thy great face, only ;
Harvest the wheat of Ohio, Illinois, Wisconsin—every
   barbed spear, under thee ;
Harvest the maize of Missouri, Kentucky, Tennessee—
   each ear in its light-green sheath,
Gather the hay to its myriad mows, in the odorous,
   tranquil barns,
Oats to their bins—the white potato, the buckwheat of
   Michigan, to theirs ;
Gather the cotton in Mississippi or Alabama—dig and
   hoard the golden, the sweet potato of Georgia
   and the Carolinas,
Clip the wool of California or Pennsylvania,
Cut the flax in the Middle States, or hemp, or tobacco
   in the Borders,
Pick the pea and the bean, or pull apples from the
   trees, or bunches of grapes from the vines,
Or aught that ripens in all These States, or North or
   South,
Under the beaming sun, and under Thee.

THE SINGER IN THE PRISON.

1

O sight of shame, and pain, and dole!
O fearful thought—a convict Soul!

RANG the refrain along the hall, the prison,
Rose to the roof, the vaults of heaven above,
Pouring in floods of melody, in tones so pensive, sweet
    and strong, the like whereof was never heard,
Reaching the far-off sentry, and the armed guards, who
    ceas'd their pacing,
Making the hearer's pulses stop for extasy and awe.

2

O sight of pity, gloom, and dole!
O pardon me, a hapless Soul!

The sun was low in the west one winter day,
When down a narrow aisle, amid the thieves and out-
    laws of the land,
(There by the hundreds seated, sear-faced murderers,
    wily counterfeiters,
Gather'd to Sunday church in prison walls—the keep-
    ers round,
Plenteous, well-arm'd, watching, with vigilant eyes,)
All that dark, cankerous blotch, a nation's criminal
    mass,
Calmly a Lady walk'd, holding a little innocent child
    by either hand,
Whom, seating on their stools beside her on the plat-
    form,
She, first preluding with the instrument, a low and
    musical prelude,
In voice surpassing all, sang forth a quaint old
    hymn.

3

THE HYMN.

A Soul, confined by bars and bands,
Cries, Help! O help! and wrings her hands;
Blinded her eyes—bleeding her breast,
Nor pardon finds, nor balm of rest.

O sight of shame, and pain, and dole!
O fearful thought—a convict Soul!

Ceaseless, she paces to and fro;
O heart-sick days! O nights of wo!
Nor hand of friend, nor loving face;
Nor favor comes, nor word of grace.

O sight of pity, gloom, and dole!
O pardon me, a hapless Soul!

It was not I that sinn'd the sin,
The ruthless Body dragg'd me in;
Though long I strove courageously,
The Body was too much for me.

O Life! no life, but bitter dole!
O burning, beaten, baffled Soul!

(Dear prison'd Soul, bear up a space,
For soon or late the certain grace;
To set thee free, and bear thee home,
The Heavenly Pardoner, Death shall come.

Convict no more—nor shame, nor dole!
Depart! a God-enfranchis'd Soul!)

4

The singer ceas'd;
One glance swept from her clear, calm eyes, o'er all
    those up-turn'd faces;
Strange sea of prison faces—a thousand varied, crafty,
    brutal, seam'd and beauteous faces:

Then rising, passing back along the narrow aisle be-
      tween them,
While her gown touch'd them, rustling in the silence,
She vanish'd with her children in the dusk.

5

While upon all, convicts and armed keepers, ere they
      stirr'd,
(Convict forgetting prison, keeper his loaded pistol,)
A hush and pause fell down, a wondrous minute,
With deep, half-stifled sobs, and sound of bad men
      bow'd, and moved to weeping,
And youth's convulsive breathings, memories of home,
The mother's voice in lullaby, the sister's care, the
      happy childhood,
The long-pent spirit rous'd to reminiscence ;
—A wondrous minute then—But after, in the solitary
      night, to many, many there,
Years after—even in the hour of death—the sad refrain
      —the tune, the voice, the words,
Resumed—the large, calm Lady walks the narrow aisle,
The wailing melody again—the singer in the prison
      sings :

> *O sight of shame, and pain, and dole !*
> *O fearful thought—a convict Soul !*

WARBLE FOR LILAC TIME.

Warble me now, for joy of Lilac-time,
Sort me, O tongue and lips, for Nature's sake, and
      sweet life's sake—and death's the same as life's,
Souvenirs of earliest summer—birds' eggs, and the first
      berries ;
Gather the welcome signs, (as children, with pebbles, or
      stringing shells ;)
Put in April and May—the hylas croaking in the ponds
      —the elastic air,

Bees, butterflies, the sparrow with its simple notes,
Blue-bird, and darting swallow—nor forget the high-
hole flashing his golden wings,
The tranquil sunny haze, the clinging smoke, the vapor,
Spiritual, airy insects, humming on gossamer wings,
Shimmer of waters, with fish in them—the cerulean
above ;
All that is jocund and sparkling—the brooks running,
The maple woods, the crisp February days, and the
sugar-making ;
The robin, where he hops, bright-eyed, brown-breasted,
With musical clear call at sunrise, and again at sunset,
Or flitting among the trees of the apple-orchard, build-
ing the nest of his mate ;
The melted snow of March—the willow sending forth
its yellow-green sprouts ;
—For spring-time is here! the summer is here! and
what is this in it and from it ?
Thou, Soul, unloosen'd—the restlessness after I know
not what ;
Come! let us lag here no longer—let us be up and
away!
O for another world! O if one could but fly like a
bird!
O to escape—to sail forth, as in a ship!
To glide with thee, O Soul, o'er all, in all, as a ship o'er
the waters !
—Gathering these hints, these preludes—the blue sky,
the grass, the morning drops of dew ;
(With additional songs—every spring will I now strike
up additional songs,
Nor ever again forget, these tender days, the chants of
Death as well as Life ;)
The lilac-scent, the bushes, and the dark green, heart-
shaped leaves,
Wood violets, the little delicate pale blossoms called
innocence,
Samples and sorts not for themselves alone, but for
their atmosphere,
To tally, drench'd with them, tested by them,
Cities and artificial life, and all their sights and scenes,

My mind henceforth, and all its meditations—my reci-
    tatives,
My land, my age, my race, for once to serve in songs,
(Sprouts, tokens ever of death indeed the same as life,)
To grace the bush I love—to sing with the birds,
A warble for joy of Lilac-time.

Who Learns My Lesson Complete?

[1] Who learns my lesson complete?
Boss, journeyman, apprentice—churchman and atheist,
The stupid and the wise thinker—parents and offspring
    —merchant, clerk, porter and customer,
Editor, author, artist, and schoolboy—Draw nigh and
    commence ;
It is no lesson—it lets down the bars to a good lesson,
And that to another, and every one to another still.

[2] The great laws take and effuse without argument ;
I am of the same style, for I am their friend,
I love them quits and quits—I do not halt, and make
    salaams.

[3] I lie abstracted, and hear beautiful tales of things,
    and the reasons of things ;
They are so beautiful, I nudge myself to listen.

[4] I cannot say to any person what I hear—I cannot say
    it to myself—it is very wonderful.

[5] It is no small matter, this round and delicious globe,
    moving so exactly in its orbit forever and ever,
    without one jolt, or the untruth of a single
    second ;
I do not think it was made in six days, nor in ten
    thousand years, nor ten billions of years,
Nor plann'd and built one thing after another, as an
    architect plans and builds a house.

⁶ I do not think seventy years is the time of a man or
    woman,
Nor that seventy millions of years is the time of a man
    or woman,
Nor that years will ever stop the existence of me, or
    any one else.

⁷ Is it wonderful that I should be immortal? as every
    one is immortal ;
I know it is wonderful, but my eyesight is equally won-
    derful, and how I was conceived in my mother's
    womb is equally wonderful ;
And pass'd from a babe, in the creeping trance of a
    couple of summers and winters, to articulate and
    walk—All this is equally wonderful.

⁸ And that my Soul embraces you this hour, and we
    affect each other without ever seeing each other,
    and never perhaps to see each other, is every bit
    as wonderful.

⁹ And that I can think such thoughts as these, is just
    as wonderful ;
And that I can remind you, and you think them, and
    know them to be true, is just as wonderful.

¹⁰ And that the moon spins round the earth, and on
    with the earth, is equally wonderful,
And that they balance themselves with the sun and
    stars, is equally wonderful.

THOUGHT.

OF Justice—As if Justice could be anything but the
    same ample law, expounded by natural judges
    and saviors,
As if it might be this thing or that thing, according to
    decisions.

MYSELF AND MINE.

[1] MYSELF and mine gymnastic ever,
To stand the cold or heat—to take good aim with a
    gun—to sail a boat—to manage horses—to be-
    get superb children,
To speak readily and clearly—to feel at home among
    common people,
And to hold our own in terrible positions, on land and
    sea.

[2] Not for an embroiderer ;
(There will always be plenty of embroiderers—I wel-
    come them also ;)
But for the fibrè of things, and for inherent men and
    women.

[3] Not to chisel ornaments,
But to chisel with free stroke the heads and limbs of
    plenteous Supreme Gods, that The States may
    realize them, walking and talking.

[4] Let me have my own way ;
Let others promulge the laws—I will make no account
    of the laws ;
Let others praise eminent men and hold up peace—I
    hold up agitation and conflict ;
I praise no eminent man—I rebuke to his face the one
    that was thought most worthy.

[5] (Who are you ? you mean devil ! And what are you
    secretly guilty of, all your life ?
Will you turn aside all your life ? Will you grub and
    chatter all your life ?)

[6] (And who are you—blabbing by rote, years, pages,
    languages, reminiscences,
Unwitting to-day that you do not know how to speak a
    single word ?)

⁷ Let others finish specimens—I never finish specimens ;
I shower them by exhaustless laws, as Nature does,
    fresh and modern continually.

⁸ I give nothing as duties ;
What others give as duties, I give as living impulses ;
(Shall I give the heart's action as a duty?)

⁹ Let others dispose of questions—I dispose of nothing
    —I arouse unanswerable questions ;
Who are they I see and touch, and what about them ?
What about these likes of myself, that draw me so close
    by tender directions and indirections ?

¹⁰ I call to the world to distrust the accounts of my
    friends, but listen to my enemies—as I myself
    do ;
I charge you, too, forever, reject those who would ex-
    pound me—for I cannot expound myself ;
I charge that there be no theory or school founded out
    of me ;
I charge you to leave all free, as I have left all free.

¹¹ After me, vista !
O, I see life is not short, but immeasurably long ;
I henceforth tread the world, chaste, temperate, an
    early riser, a steady grower,
Every hour the semen of centuries—and still of centu-
    ries.

¹² I will follow up these continual lessons of the air,
    water, earth ;
I perceive I have no time to lose.

TO OLD AGE.

I SEE in you the estuary that enlarges and spreads itself
    grandly as it pours in the great Sea.

MIRACLES.

[1] Why! who makes much of a miracle?
As to me, I know of nothing else but miracles,
Whether I walk the streets of Manhattan,
Or dart my sight over the roofs of houses toward the
　　sky,
Or wade with naked feet along the beach, just in the
　　edge of the water,
Or stand under trees in the woods,
Or talk by day with any one I love—or sleep in the bed
　　at night with any one I love,
Or sit at table at dinner with the rest,
Or look at strangers opposite me riding in the car,
Or watch honey-bees busy around the hive, of a sum-
　　mer forenoon,
Or animals feeding in the fields,
Or birds—or the wonderfulness of insects in the air,
Or the wonderfulness of the sun-down—or of stars
　　shining so quiet and bright,
Or the exquisite, delicate, thin curve of the new moon
　　in spring ;
Or whether I go among those I like best, and that like
　　me best—mechanics, boatmen, farmers,
Or among the savans — or to the soiree — or to the
　　opera,
Or stand a long while looking at the movements of
　　machinery,
Or behold children at their sports,
Or the admirable sight of the perfect old man, or the
　　perfect old woman,
Or the sick in hospitals, or the dead carried to burial,
Or my own eyes and figure in the glass ;
These, with the rest, one and all, are to me miracles,
The whole referring — yet each distinct, and in its
　　place.

[2] To me, every hour of the light and dark is a mir-
　　acle,
Every cubic inch of space is a miracle,

Every square yard of the surface of the earth is spread
    with the same,
Every foot of the interior swarms with the same ;
Every spear of grass—the frames, limbs, organs, of men
    and women, and all that concerns them,
All these to me are unspeakably perfect miracles.

³ To me the sea is a continual miracle ;
The fishes that swim—the rocks—the motion of the
    waves—the ships, with men in them,
What stranger miracles are there?

SPARKLES FROM THE WHEEL.

1

WHERE the city's ceaseless crowd moves on, the live-
    long day,
Withdrawn, I join a group of children watching—I
    pause aside with them.

By the curb, toward the edge of the flagging,
A knife-grinder works at his wheel, sharpening a great
    knife ;
Bending over, he carefully holds it to the stone—by
    foot and knee,
With measur'd tread, he turns rapidly—As he presses
    with light but firm hand,
Forth issue, then, in copious golden jets,
Sparkles from the wheel.

2

The scene, and all its belongings—how they seize and
    affect me !
The sad, sharp-chinn'd old man, with worn clothes, and
    broad shoulder-band of leather ;
Myself, effusing and fluid—a phantom curiously float-
    ing—now here absorb'd and arrested ;

The group, (an unminded point, set in a vast surround-
    ing ;)
The attentive, quiet children—the loud, proud, restive
    base of the streets ;
The low, hoarse purr of the whirling stone—the light-
    press'd blade,
Diffusing, dropping, sideways-darting, in tiny showers
    of gold,
Sparkles from the wheel.

EXCELSIOR.

Who has gone farthest? For lo! have not I gone far-
    ther?
And who has been just? For I would be the most just
    person of the earth ;
And who most cautious? For I would be more cau-
    tious ;
And who has been happiest? O I think it is I! I think
    no one was ever happier than I ;
And who has lavish'd all? For I lavish constantly the
    best I have ;
And who has been firmest? For I would be firmer ;
And who proudest? For I think I have reason to be
    the proudest son alive—for I am the son of the
    brawny and tall-topt city ;
And who has been bold and true? For I would be the
    boldest and truest being of the universe ;
And who benevolent? For I would show more benevo-
    lence than all the rest ;
And who has projected beautiful words through the
    longest time? Have I not outvied him? have I
    not said the words that shall stretch through
    longer time ?
And who has receiv'd the love of the most friends? For
    I know what it is to receive the passionate love
    of many friends ;

And who possesses a perfect and enamour'd body ? For
I do not believe any one possesses a more perfect
or enamour'd body than mine ;
And who thinks the amplest thoughts ? For I will sur-
round those thoughts ;
And who has made hymns fit for the earth? For I am
mad with devouring extasy to make joyous hymns
for the whole earth !

Mediums.

They shall arise in the States ;
They shall report Nature, laws, physiology, and happiness ;
They shall illustrate Democracy and the kosmos ;
They shall be alimentive, amative, perceptive ;
They shall be complete women and men—their pose
brawny and supple, their drink water, their
blood clean and clear ;
They shall enjoy materialism and the sight of products
—they shall enjoy the sight of the beef, lumber,
bread-stuffs, of Chicago, the great city ;
They shall train themselves to go in public to become
orators and oratresses ;
Strong and sweet shall their tongues be—poems and
materials of poems shall come from their lives—
they shall be makers and finders ;
Of them, and of their works, shall emerge divine con-
veyers, to convey gospels ;
Characters, events, retrospections, shall be convey'd in
gospels—Trees, animals, waters, shall be convey'd,
Death, the future, the invisible faith, shall all be convey'd.

KOSMOS.

WHO includes diversity, and is Nature,
Who is the amplitude of the earth, and the coarseness
    and sexuality of the earth, and the great charity
    of the earth, and the equilibrium also,
Who has not look'd forth from the windows, the eyes,
    for nothing, or whose brain held audience with
    messengers for nothing ;
Who contains believers and disbelievers—Who is the
    most majestic lover ;
Who holds duly his or her triune proportion of real-
    ism, spiritualism, and of the æsthetic, or intel-
    lectual,
Who, having consider'd the Body, finds all its organs
    and parts good ;
Who, out of the theory of the earth, and of his or her
    body, understands by subtle analogies all other
    theories,
The theory of a city, a poem, and of the large politics
    of These States ;
Who believes not only in our globe, with its sun and
    moon, but in other globes, with their suns and
    moons ;
Who, constructing the house of himself or herself, not
    for a day, but for all time, sees races, eras, dates,
    generations,
The past, the future, dwelling there, like space, insep-
    arable together.

TO A PUPIL.

[1] Is reform needed ? Is it through you ?
The greater the reform needed, the greater the person-
    ality you need to accomplish it.

[2] You ! do you not see how it would serve to have eyes,
    blood, complexion, clean and sweet ?

Do you not see how it would serve to have such a Body
and Soul, that when you enter the crowd, an
atmosphere of desire and command enters with
you, and every one is impress'd with your personality?

[3] O the magnet! the flesh over and over!
Go, dear friend! if need be, give up all else, and commence to-day to inure yourself to pluck, reality,
self-esteem, definiteness, elevatedness;
Rest not, till you rivet and publish yourself of your
own personality.

WHAT AM I, AFTER ALL.

[1] WHAT am I, after all, but a child, pleas'd with the
sound of my own name? repeating it over and
over;
I stand apart to hear—it never tires me.

[2] To you, your name also;
Did you think there was nothing but two or three pro-
nunciations in the sound of your name?

OTHERS MAY PRAISE WHAT THEY LIKE.

OTHERS may praise what they like;
But I, from the banks of the running Missouri, praise
nothing, in art, or aught else,
Till it has well inhaled the atmosphere of this river—
also the western prairie-scent,
And fully exudes it again.

☞ *To any Hospital or School-Founder, or Public Beneficiary, anywhere.*

BROTHER OF ALL, WITH GENEROUS HAND.

(G. P., Buried February, 1870.)

1

¹ BROTHER of all, with generous hand,
Of thee, pondering on thee, as o'er thy tomb, I and my
    Soul,
A thought to launch in memory of thee,
A burial verse for thee.

² What may we chant, O thou within this tomb?
What tablets, pictures, hang for thee, O millionaire?
—The life thou lived'st we know not,
But that thou walk'dst thy years in barter, 'mid the
    haunts of brokers ;
Nor heroism thine, nor war, nor glory.

³ Yet lingering, yearning, joining soul with thine,
If not thy past we chant, we chant the future,
Select, adorn the future.

2

⁴ Lo, Soul, the graves of heroes !
The pride of lands—the gratitudes of men,
The statues of the manifold famous dead, Old World
    and New,
The kings, inventors, generals, poets, (stretch wide thy
    vision, Soul,)
The excellent rulers of the races, great discoverers,
    sailors,
Marble and brass select from them, with pictures,
    scenes,
(The histories of the lands, the races, bodied there,
In what they've built for, graced and graved,
Monuments to their heroes.)

3

⁵ Silent, my Soul,
With drooping lids, as waiting, ponder'd,
Turning from all the samples, all the monuments of
  heroes.

⁶ While through the interior vistas,
Noiseless uprose, phantasmic, (as, by night, Auroras of
  the North,)
Lambent tableaux, prophetic, bodiless scenes,
Spiritual projections.

⁷ In one, among the city streets, a laborer's home appear'd,
After his day's work done, cleanly, sweet-air'd, the gas-
  light burning,
The carpet swept, and a fire in the cheerful stove.

⁸ In one, the sacred parturition scene,
A happy, painless mother birth'd a perfect child.

⁹ In one, at a bounteous morning meal,
Sat peaceful parents, with contented sons.

¹⁰ In one, by twos and threes, young people,
Hundreds concentering, walk'd the paths and streets
  and roads,
Toward a tall-domed school.

¹¹ In one a trio, beautiful,
Grandmother, loving daughter, loving daughter's
  daughter, sat,
Chatting and sewing.

¹² In one, along a suite of noble rooms,
'Mid plenteous books and journals, paintings on the
  walls, fine statuettes,
Were groups of friendly journeymen, mechanics, young
  and old,
Reading, conversing.

[13] All, all the shows of laboring life,
City and country, women's, men's and children's,
Their wants provided for, hued in the sun, and tinged
          for once with joy,
Marriage, the street, the factory, farm, the house-room,
          lodging-room,
Labor and toil, the bath, gymnasium, play-ground,
          library, college,
The student, boy or girl, led forward to be taught ;
The sick cared for, the shoeless shod—the orphan
          father'd and mother'd,
The hungry fed, the houseless housed ;
(The intentions perfect and divine,
The workings, details, haply human.)

4

[11] O thou within this tomb,
From thee, such scenes—thou stintless, lavish Giver,
Tallying the gifts of Earth—large as the Earth,
Thy name an Earth, with mountains, fields and rivers.

[15] Nor by your streams alone, you rivers,
By you, your banks, Connecticut,
By you, and all your teeming life, Old Thames,
By you, Potomac, laving the ground Washington trod
          —by you Patapsco,
You, Hudson—you, endless Mississippi—not by you
          alone,
But to the high seas launch, my thought, his memory.

5

[16] Lo, Soul, by this tomb's lambency,
The darkness of the arrogant standards of the world,
With all its flaunting aims, ambitions, pleasures.

[17] (Old, commonplace, and rusty saws,
The rich, the gay, the supercilious, smiled at long,
Now, piercing to the marrow in my bones,
Fused with each drop my heart's blood jets,
Swim in ineffable meaning.)

[18] Lo, Soul, the sphere requireth, portioneth,
To each his share, his measure,
The moderate to the moderate, the ample to the
    ample.

[19] Lo, Soul, see'st thou not, plain as the sun,
The only real wealth of wealth in generosity,
The only life of life in goodness?

NIGHT ON THE PRAIRIES.

[1] NIGHT on the prairies;
The supper is over—the fire on the ground burns low;
The wearied emigrants sleep, wrapt in their blankets:
I walk by myself—I stand and look at the stars, which
    I think now I never realized before.

[2] Now I absorb immortality and peace,
I admire death, and test propositions.

[3] How plenteous! How spiritual! How resumé!
The same Old Man and Soul—the same old aspirations,
    and the same content.

[4] I was thinking the day most splendid, till I saw what
    the not-day exhibited,
I was thinking this globe enough, till there sprang out
    so noiseless around me myriads of other globes.

[5] Now, while the great thoughts of space and eternity
    fill me, I will measure myself by them;
And now, touch'd with the lives of other globes, arrived
    as far along as those of the earth,
Or waiting to arrive, or pass'd on farther than those of
    the earth.

I henceforth no more ignore them, than I ignore my
    own life,
Or the lives of the earth arrived as far as mine, or
    waiting to arrive.

6 O I see now that life cannot exhibit all to me—as the
    day cannot,
I see that I am to wait for what will be exhibited by
    death.

ON JOURNEYS THROUGH THE STATES.

1 On journeys through the States we start,
(Ay, through the world—urged by these songs,
Sailing henceforth to every land—to every sea ;)
We, willing learners of all, teachers of all, and lovers
    of all.

2 We have watch'd the seasons dispensing themselves,
    and passing on,
We have said, Why should not a man or woman do as
    much as the seasons, and effuse as much ?

3 We dwell a while in every city and town ;
We pass through Kanada, the north-east, the vast valley
    of the Mississippi, and the Southern States ;
We confer on equal terms with each of The States,
We make trial of ourselves, and invite men and women
    to hear ;
We say to ourselves, Remember, fear not, be candid,
    promulge the body and the Soul ;
Dwell a while and pass on—Be copious, temperate,
    chaste, magnetic,
And what you effuse may then return as the seasons
    return,
And may be just as much as the seasons.

SAVANTISM.

THITHER, as I look, I see each result and glory retracing
    itself and nestling close, always obligated ;
Thither hours, months, years—thither trades, compacts,
    establishments, even the most minute ;
Thither every-day life, speech, utensils, politics, per-
    sons, estates ;
Thither we also, I with my leaves and songs, trustful,
    admirant,
As a father, to his father going, takes his children
    along with him.

LOCATIONS AND TIMES.

LOCATIONS and times—what is it in me that meets them
    all, whenever and wherever, and makes me at
    home ?
Forms, colors, densities, odors—what is it in me that
    corresponds with them ?

THOUGHT.

OF Equality—As if it harm'd me, giving others the
    same chances and rights as myself—As if it
    were not indispensable to my own rights that
    others possess the same.

OFFERINGS.

A THOUSAND perfect men and women appear,
Around each gathers a cluster of friends, and gay chil-
    dren and youths, with offerings.

TESTS.

All submit to them, where they sit, inner, secure,
    unapproachable to analysis, in the Soul ;
Not traditions—not the outer authorities are the judges
    —they are the judges of outer authorities, and
    of all traditions ;
They corroborate as they go, only whatever corrobo-
    rates themselves, and touches themselves ;
For all that, they have it forever in themselves to cor-
    roborate far and near, without one exception.

THE TORCH.

On my northwest coast in the midst of the night, a
    fishermen's group stands watching ;
Out on the lake, that expands before them, others are
    spearing salmon ;
The canoe, a dim shadowy thing, moves across the
    black water,
Bearing a Torch a-blaze at the prow.

TO YOU.

Let us twain walk aside from the rest ;
Now we are together privately, do you discard cere-
    mony ;
Come! vouchsafe to me what has yet been vouchsafed
    to none—Tell me the whole story,
Let us talk of death—unbosom all freely,
Tell me what you would not tell your brother, wife,
    husband, or physician.

GODS.

1

Thought of the Infinite—the All!
Be thou my God.

2

Lover Divine, and Perfect Comrade!
Waiting, content, invisible yet, but certain,
Be thou my God.

3

Thou—thou, the Ideal Man!
Fair, able, beautiful, content, and loving,
Complete in Body, and dilate in Spirit,
Be thou my God.

4

O Death—(for Life has served its turn;)
Opener and usher to the heavenly mansion!
Be thou my God.

5

Aught, aught, of mightiest, best, I see, conceive, or
    know,
(To break the stagnant tie—thee, thee to free, O Soul,)
Be thou my God.

6

Or thee, Old Cause, whene'er advancing;
All great Ideas, the races' aspirations,
All that exalts, releases thee, my Soul!
All heroisms, deeds of rapt enthusiasts,
Be ye my Gods!

7

Or Time and Space!
Or shape of Earth, divine and wondrous!
Or shape in I myself—or some fair shape, I, viewing,
    worship,
Or lustrous orb of sun, or star by night,
Be ye my Gods.

TO ONE SHORTLY TO DIE.

1

[1] FROM all the rest I single out you, having a message
    for you :
You are to die—Let others tell you what they please, I
    cannot prevaricate,
I am exact and merciless, but I love you—There is no
    escape for you.

[2] Softly I lay my right hand upon you—you just feel it,
I do not argue—I bend my head close, and half en-
    velop it,
I sit quietly by—I remain faithful,
I am more than nurse, more than parent or neighbor,
I absolve you from all except yourself, spiritual, bodily
    —that is eternal—you yourself will surely escape,
The corpse you will leave will be but excrementitious.

2

[3] The sun bursts through in unlooked-for directions!
Strong thoughts fill you, and confidence—you smile!
You forget you are sick, as I forget you are sick,
You do not see the medicines—you do not mind the
    weeping friends—I am with you,
I exclude others from you—there is nothing to be com-
    miserated,
I do not commiserate—I congratulate you.

Now Finale to the Shore.

NOW FINALE TO THE SHORE.

Now finale to the shore!
Now, land and life, finale, and farewell!
Now Voyager depart! (much, much for thee is yet in
    store ;)
Often enough hast thou adventur'd o'er the seas,
Cautiously cruising, studying the charts,
Duly again to port, and hawser's tie, returning :
—But now obey thy cherish'd, secret wish,
Embrace thy friends—leave all in order ;
To port, and hawser's tie, no more returning,
Depart upon thy endless cruise, old Sailor!

SHUT NOT YOUR DOORS, &c.

Shut not your doors to me, proud libraries,
For that which was lacking on all your well-fill'd
    shelves, yet needed most, I bring ;
Forth from the army, the war emerging—a book I
    have made,
The words of my book nothing—the drift of it every-
    thing ;

A book separate, not link'd with the rest, nor felt by
    the intellect,
But you, ye untold latencies, will thrill to every page ;
Through Space and Time fused in a chant, and the
    flowing, eternal Identity,
To Nature, encompassing these, encompassing God—
    to the joyous, electric All,
To the sense of Death—and accepting, exulting in
    Death, in its turn, the same as life,
The entrance of Man I sing.

THOUGHT.

As they draw to a close,
Of what underlies the precedent songs—of my aims in
    them ;
Of the seed I have sought to plant in them ;
Of joy, sweet joy, through many a year, in them ;
(For them—for them have I lived—In them my work
    is done ;)
Of many an aspiration fond—of many a dream and
    plan,
Of you, O mystery great!—to place on record faith in
    you, O death !
—To compact you, ye parted, diverse lives !
To put rapport the mountains, and rocks, and streams,
And the winds of the north, and the forests of oak and
    pine,
With you, O soul of man.

THE UNTOLD WANT.

THE untold want, by life and land ne'er granted,
Now, Voyager, sail thou forth, to seek and find.

PORTALS.

What are those of the known, but to ascend and enter
the Unknown ?
And what are those of life, but for Death ?

THESE CAROLS.

These Carols, sung to cheer my passage through the
world I see,
For completion, I dedicate to the Invisible World.

THIS DAY, O SOUL.

This day, O Soul, I give you a wondrous mirror ;
Long in the dark, in tarnish and cloud it lay—But the
cloud has pass'd, and the tarnish gone ;
... Behold, O Soul! it is now a clean and bright mir-
ror,
Faithfully showing you all the things of the world.

WHAT PLACE IS BESIEGED?

What place is besieged, and vainly tries to raise the
siege ?
Lo! I send to that place a commander, swift, brave,
immortal ;
And with him horse and foot—and parks of artillery,
And artillery-men, the deadliest that ever fired gun.

TO THE READER AT PARTING.

Now, dearest comrade, lift me to your face,
We must separate awhile—Here! take from my lips
     this kiss ;
Whoever you are, I give it especially to you ;
So long !—And I hope we shall meet again.

JOY, SHIPMATE, JOY!

Joy ! shipmate—joy !
(Pleas'd to my Soul at death I cry ;)
Our life is closed—our life begins ;
The long, long anchorage we leave,
The ship is clear at last—she leaps !
She swiftly courses from the shore ;
Joy ! shipmate—joy !

LaVergne, TN USA
25 January 2011
213906LV00002B/34/A